# A soldier's mother

Rheta Childe Dorr

**Alpha Editions**

This edition published in 2023

ISBN : 9789357966641

Design and Setting By
**Alpha Editions**
www.alphaedis.com
Email - info@alphaedis.com

# Contents

# CHAPTER I
# WHERE THE LONG TRAIL LED

ON THE lapel of my coat I wear a little pin, a pin with a single star, ruby red on a bar of white. My only son is a member of the American Expeditionary Force in France. More than a million American women wear pins like mine. Some have two stars, three, even four, and every one covers a heart heavy with anxiety and foreboding. That little service pin which mothers wear, fathers, too; sisters, sweethearts, wives, is a symbol of sacrifice. It should be something more than that.

My star has come to mean love of country far surpassing the mild patriotism of other days. It means confidence and courage for whatever in these tragic times I shall need courage. It means pride in the young manhood of America and hope unbounded for the future of America, which lies in their hands. Before I went to France I wore my service pin for one soldier—my son. I wear it now for the American army. If I can, by writing of that army as I have just seen it in France, lessen a little for other women the burden of anxiety and dread I shall count my journey worth while.

I went to France as a correspondent, a reporter, to write about the war. I was sent, not because I am a woman, but in spite of the fact, and merely because my editors believed that I could handle that particular job. My letter of credentials to the French Foreign Office said that I had reported the Russian revolution for my paper and that I was now assigned to France with the view of informing readers in the United States as to participation of United States troops in war and the political situations of the allied countries in the war.

I hope that my editors' confidence in me was not entirely misplaced and that I did not quite fall down on my job. But what I experienced in France and what I brought out with me were not exactly what I had expected. I went to France as a correspondent, deeply interested in my work, but very soon after I arrived and almost with my first contact with our marvelous new army I forgot all about my work. I forgot that I was in France after military and political facts.

I forgot that I was a correspondent. I was conscious only that I was a mother. The mother of a boy in France. I was one in heart with a million other American women I have never seen and will never see; one with every woman in the land who wears a service pin.

*I discovered that try as I might to think of armies, strategies and diplomacies, the only thing that vitally concerned me in France was to find out how my son was faring, and in doing so I was finding out the things that other mothers wanted to know about their boys.*

Where they are, how they live, who their comrades are, how they work and play, what they are learning, how they get along with their strange new neighbors, the French people, and what the war is doing to their minds and souls, as well as their bodies. I wanted, fervently, to know all this about one soldier, and I believed that the other women would like to know about their own.

Our soldiers are more than three thousand miles away from home, and they have gone on a terrible errand. We know less about war than any other women in the world, but we know that it is a brutal, pitiless, bloodthirsty business. We know that bodies perish in war, and sometimes souls, which is worse. Going over in the steamer a horrible story was told me, a story which turned out to be quite untrue, but which when I heard it cost me a sleepless night. It was to the effect that vice was so rampant in all the armies that a whole shipload of hopelessly diseased Australian soldiers had recently sailed from England. The hospitals had salvaged many, it was said, but these men, who had left home clean, wholesome, decent boys, were now being sent back to die, physical and moral wrecks. Some, it was certain, would commit suicide during the voyage.

That tale filled me with such terror that I went to some lengths to investigate it. It was quite untrue, and I repeat it here only because it is representative of stories that are current everywhere and add greatly to the sufferings of the women at home. *The first thing I want to say about our army is that the men are morally as safe in France as they could possibly be at home. I made it my particular business to know it.*

I spent three months in France, traveling over most of the considerable territory occupied by the American forces. I visited something like twenty-five camps, small ones, large ones and immense ones, where the men are training, where they are being made into experts in special lines of fighting; where they are at work building miles of wharves, warehouses, cold storage plants, barracks and hospitals; where they are laying railroads and dredging rivers; where they are performing marvels of constructive work necessary to the life of an army far removed from its base.

I met and talked with thousands of soldiers in their camps, in the Y. M. C. A. and Red Cross canteens, in many ancient towns of central France. I saw our men disembarking from their transports, and I saw them tramping through ice-cold mud to the front-line trenches. I talked with them in their billets in lonely little villages of the north, and in vacation cities of the azure south. I have visited American soldiers in hospitals and I have knelt beside their graves. *Our soldiers have only one enemy, and that is the Germans.* That enemy they must fight and conquer, and we over here must steel our hearts to the sacrifices of life, the suffering and maiming that are absolutely inevitable and will have to be borne. The casualty lists, every day growing a little longer, are bound to grow even longer. What English mothers and French mothers, what all the people of all the warring nations have endured, we shall have to endure. It is the world's pain and we can not escape it.

What we Americans have to help us bear what is coming in the next few months is the knowledge that our losses are going to be as few as possible. Life is to be safeguarded as far as human agencies can devise. Our army is organized for that. Men are not to be sacrificed unnecessarily. The best science in the world is being mobilized to save suffering and to heal wounds. Sickness and accident are being guarded against. Drunkenness and immorality are under strictest ban.

Some of this I was privileged to hear from the man who perhaps more than any other individual is responsible for the lives and the souls of our men in France, General Pershing. I saw him twice, once briefly in Paris, where he talked to me five minutes before leaving for an allied war council at Versailles, and once at length in his headquarters in a quaint old town which is the general headquarters of the staff of our army in France.

General Pershing is the least formal of any great officer I have ever seen, with the notable exception of "Papa" Joffre, but generals are all very important personages and have to be addressed with circumspection. I wanted very much to say to General Pershing, but of course I didn't, that after seeing him I felt a whole lot easier about my especial soldier. A more human commanding officer, one more concerned about the last detail of the life of the enlisted man, I am sure never lived. He spoke of the soldiers as a father speaks of his sons, with pride and passionate concern.

*"They are the best in the world," he said, and he added that although our talk was private and that he could not be quoted, I was at liberty to repeat those words: "Our soldiers are fine men, clean, strong, intelligent, and they will make magnificent fighters. Tell the people at home, especially the mothers, that they can be proud of their men. Tell them that almost without exception their behavior is beyond criticism. Tell them that for me."*

Proud of their commander also may the American people be, and over and above all, proud of the cause for which the American soldiers fight and for which they are ready to die. Not in the whole history of the world has a more righteous war been fought. I do not think the majority of Americans yet dream of the depth of depravity contemplated by the men who brought about the war. We have heard of German atrocities and we have shuddered at the recital.

But the plan and object of this war on the part of those Prussians who are responsible for it constitute the worst atrocity of all, for the plan was the murder of Christian civilization and the object was the enslavement of mankind.

I have seen some of the effects of a partial success of the German war lords' plan, and I, the mother of a soldier on the French front, say to the mothers of other soldiers that I would be ashamed to have him anywhere else. Not long before leaving France I saw him for a short hour, a simple enlisted man in a humble post of duty. The spring wind blowing over the devastated and ravished plains bore the roaring of artillery plainly to our ears. Every day since then those guns have roared nearer, and now that part of France is closed to civilians.

The next message that came out of the sector where the Americans hold the line brought mourning and tears to many women. And yet I can truthfully say that I would be happier to have my son dead in France, sleeping in a soldier's grave beyond the sea, than to have him alive and safe, shirking his duty in a bullet-proof job at home.

I do not believe that in the years to come there is going to be much happiness for the men who are shirking, nor for the women who may be encouraging them to shirk. The shirkers are going to play a very pitiful part in the national life of this country after the war. The men who come home will be the rulers of America's future destiny. They will be the strong builders of our greatness. They are learning in this war how to build.

# CHAPTER II
# I ADOPT THE AMERICAN ARMY

LOOKING back over my three months in France, most of the time spent in visiting American military camps, some experiences stand out above all others. One, a precious personal experience, gave me my first insight into the splendid idealism and individual worth of the enlisted men of our army. I had gone to France a newspaper correspondent, without a single plan, without even a hope of seeing my soldier son. I had no intention of using my privileged position to seek him out. I did not know where he was, nor did I ask.

The American soldier abroad is theoretically still in America. He gets his letters through an American branch post-office in Paris, and they are sent to him in care of his regiment and his company, with no more definite address than "American Expeditionary Force." My son knew my Paris address, but he could not, even had he wished to do so, tell me his.

With a few thousand more impatient youngsters my boy had enlisted before the draft, fearing that he might draw a late number. He signed up on the day when I sailed for Russia, and he was in France nearly two months before I returned to the United States. Thus our separation had been a longer one than was usual in this war. So when he wrote me in February that he had been given a week's leave and hoped to be sent to Aix-les-Bains, I hoped so too most fervently, because I had been ordered to Aix-les-Bains to write the story of the first vacation of our soldiers.

I arrived two days after the first contingent of men, the dried mud of the trenches caking their uniforms and their worn boots, had marched to music and cheers through the flag-draped streets of Aix. I drove directly from the station to the headquarters of the provost marshal, and asked if a certain private soldier was in town, and if so where. He was there, and a sympathetic young man in uniform of the military police searched the lists for the record of his hotel. It is part of the intelligent care taken of our soldiers overseas that even on their permissions, or leaves from duty, the highest authorities know exactly where they live and how. No mother need worry lest her son get lost in France. He can't get lost.

In two minutes I had my son's address and was on my way to the hotel. He was not there, but the black-eyed little *patronne*, also sympathetic, found me a room on his floor. It was near the luncheon hour and I sat down at the window nearest the street, eagerly scrutinizing every soldier who passed, especially those who turned in at the hotel gate. Finally a soldier came swinging down the street, and it seemed to me that he looked familiar. Yet I was not sure. Could nine months make such a difference in a boy of twenty? This one, with the absurd little tooth-brush mustache and the cap on the side of his head, was taller, broader, straighter than my son. He was more intensely alive. Yet he walked like my Julian.

I waited for him to come up-stairs, but he did not come. I decided that he had gone directly to the dining-room, so I went down-stairs and into the big room, every table of which was filled with uniformed men, eating, laughing and talking.

It was the boy. I was so overwhelmed at the sight of him that I could not take more than a step into the room. I could not speak. Something of my intense emotion must have reached him, for he looked up, saw me, and in one bound was beside me with his arms wide, just as when I used to visit him unexpectedly at school. "Mother, mother!" he cried. Instantly at the word the noisy talk and laughter stopped dead, and every man in the room sprang to his feet. It was not a tribute to me, but to their own mothers at home. Right there I adopted the American army.

I am proud to say that a small section of the American army, all of it in that hotel, adopted me. Some were too shy to come up and be introduced, but I had broad smiles whenever I met any of them, and always, when I entered the dining-room, the same chivalric greeting.

I talked with hundreds of soldiers during that week in Aix-les-Bains, and in the little town of Chambéry, two miles distant, also a vacation center for our men. It is not mere boasting to say that they are, man for man, the most amazingly fine-looking soldiers in the world. They average rather larger than the English, and broader and more muscular than either English or French.

"*Regardez donc, les épaules!*" Look at the shoulders, I have heard dozens of Frenchmen exclaim. And they might as well exclaim, look at their pink and healthy skins, their clear eyes and splendid teeth. A generation ago we were known as a nation of dyspeptics. No one in France or England will ever call us that again. Our soldiers are as nearly perfect physical specimens as any men alive.

They are remarkably intelligent. Their eyes and ears are wide open to learn all they can of the wonderful land of France, and especially of the historic past which lives in old châteaus, ruined castles and Roman remains all over France. Aix-les-Bains, as every one probably knows, is in Savoy, which was once an Italian state, but which voted itself French sometime in the eighteen-fifties. In Chambéry is an ancient château which was the seat of the former dukes of Savoy. It is a picturesque old pile, built in the thirteenth century and still habitable.

Those American soldiers overran the château, climbed the corkscrew stone staircase to the top of the tallest watch tower, swarming over the ivy-clad walls, exploring every corner of the place. They speculated on probable methods of warfare and defense in the thirteenth century, and quarreled cheerfully as to how long their regiment could have held the château against the assaults of the other fellows' regiment. They had more fun with that château than any of its original owners ever had.

They climbed mountains around Aix, taking delight in all-day hikes above the early spring snow line. They seemed thrilled at the thought that they, fresh from Iowa, North Dakota, Georgia, Texas, were actually looking across the valleys and hills at Mont Blanc and the Alps. Bicycles could be rented for about fifteen cents an hour, and hundreds of men spent their time exploring the country around. In the late afternoons and evenings they gathered in the big magnificent casino, now under lease to the Y. M. C. A., and delightfully swapped experiences.

During the entire week I never once saw a drunken or a disorderly soldier. One day at luncheon one youth who had imbibed a little too freely of *vin ordinaire*, perfectly accessible to all, and very cheap, suddenly became inspired to sing. The only thing he could think of was the doxology, and he sang one whole line of it before he was pulled back into his seat and his vocal efforts extinguished in a roar of laughter. That was the sole and only approach to rough-house I witnessed in Aix.

The healthy enjoyment and the consistent good behavior of the Americans seemed to impress the French as miraculous. Half a dozen French officers on leave in the famous watering place spent hours in the Y. M. C. A. headquarters, and townspeople brought their families to see the Americans, hear them sing *Over There*, and *Joan of Arc*, and stag dance to the music of Lieutenant Europe's famous regimental band. Europe, who used to play for idle New York to tango, has a band of colored soldiers who are going to be known all over the continent before the war ends. The men all sing as well as play, and their music is really remarkable. Whenever a colored soldier appeared on the street the French children followed him in a rapt procession. They followed all the Americans, but Europe's men had them hypnotized.

In Aix I saw the beginning of what I believe is going to be a never-ending friendship and understanding between the American people and the French. You have heard, no doubt, about how the French double the prices of everything as soon as an American soldier enters a town. Some French shopkeepers have done this, of course. The American soldier seems to be rolling in wealth, and he rarely even counts his change. The temptation to overcharge a man who throws down a fifty franc note in payment for an apple, carelessly inquiring "Is that enough," must be pretty strong. But let me tell you that avarice is not the ruling passion of the French, and their dealings with the American soldier are often marked with consideration most extraordinary.

Vacations do not come cheaply to the American soldier in France, at least the stay at Aix-les-Bains was not cheap. Every man who went there was supposed to have a minimum of one hundred and fifty francs, or twenty-seven dollars, in his possession. When he registered at the office of the provost marshal he drew a slip of paper with the name of a hotel on it. To that hotel he was obliged to go. The tariff varied from ninety-three to one hundred and twenty-eight francs for the week, and this sum, seventeen dollars and sixty-four cents to twenty-three dollars and four cents, had to be paid in advance.

A few of the soldiers failed to get this into their heads before coming, and there was considerable borrowing in the first few days. Lucky were they who had friends from whom to borrow. One tall shy youth from Georgia, I think it was Georgia, came to the Y. M. C. A. with a pathetic tale of tragedy based on the fact that he had arrived in Aix with only eighty francs in his pocket. He had probably never been twenty miles from his home village before he went to France with his regiment, and here he found himself shut out from his hotel in a strange European town, with thirteen dollars and sixty cents less than he needed to support existence.

The Y. M. C. A. secretary suggested that he go back and ask permission to stay as long as his money lasted, but the boy was too frightened and forlorn to make the venture. Besides, he spoke no French and could never explain himself to that terrible *patronne*. In France it is always the women who hold the cash-box and manage the business end of hotel keeping.

The Y. M. C. A. secretary put on his hat and went back with the drooping Georgian to plead with the *patronne*. She had not previously understood the case, and now was all kindness and sympathy.

"The poor infant!" she exclaimed. "So far away from home and only eighty francs. Wait, monsieur, until I consult my husband."

Soon she came back smiling. "It is all right, monsieur," she said. "The big infant may stay the week for eighty francs. We also have a son under the colors. May some one be a little kind to him when he needs it."

This story, I believe, is more truly typical of the spirit of the French people toward our men than any tale of extortion, however true.

# CHAPTER III
## SEEING AMERICA OVER THERE

VACATION days are always swift flying, but that vacation week I spent in Aix-les-Bains with my soldier son broke all the records for brevity. The day of departure came almost before I realized that we had been fortunate enough to meet. We left Aix within a few hours of each other, my train first. I had a last glimpse of the boy standing on the station platform waving his cap and smiling. How is it that we can smile at such moments? Perhaps only because we are a little something more than dust, because we have aspirations, dim and dreaming though they may be, beyond mortal life and love. So we went our ways toward our separate duties, he to the front, I to the rear. His task was to fight, mine to write. If he could go to his work with a smile, then I could too. And I did.

I want to visualize to the American people who have sons and brothers and husbands in this war the immensity of the work the men have undertaken. Not only the work of fighting, but of building and preparation. Fighting furnishes the most spectacular and tragic aspect of war. But that is not all there is to the great game. War is a stupendous business enterprise. It is a feat of engineering beside which the building of the Panama Canal looks like a mere pastime. When I started out to see America, as it had established itself in France, I did not dream of the greatness I was to encounter, a greatness which has fairly staggered and inspired those of our allies who have seen it.

The first anniversary of the American entrance into the world war was the occasion of what almost might be called special American editions of most of the large English and French newspapers. Columns of space in these papers were devoted to encomiums of praise of our enterprise, our ingenuity, our manifold and miraculous accomplishments in the space of twelve short months. Miraculous was a word most frequently used, miraculous and astounding.

It is too bad that the people of the United States can not at present be told all of the amazing feats of building, engineering, transportation and railroad construction which have so impressed the allies abroad. It would inspire and encourage them to know it, but unfortunately it is necessary to keep as many of the details as possible a secret from Germany. Before the fateful August day in 1914, when the vast German army started on its march across doomed Belgium, the war lords knew the French railroad system as well as they knew their own. They had maps of every foot of railroad in the

French republic. They had an accurate catalogue of French rolling stock, and they knew exactly the number and capacity of railroad manufacturing and repair shops. They probably knew the railroad men of the country down to the last patch on an engineer's overalls.

But the Germans do not know what has happened to the French railroad system since April 6, 1917, the date of our entrance into the war. Of course we do not want them to know, but I don't mind telling them that what has happened deserves the adjectives lavished on us by the English and French newspapers. I have been over hundreds of miles of that part of the French railroad system which moves our men and their supplies from ocean ports to the fighting front, and I agree with Secretary Baker when he said, on his departure from France, that what had been accomplished was inspiring to behold.

I shall never forget a Sunday that I spent at a railroad station in a town in central France. The town, which can not be named, is a small and not very important manufacturing city, but it is now one of the important junctions in the chain of railroads leading from the southwestern and northwestern seaports to the battle-front of the northeast.

The day was Sunday, just three days after the great push of March twenty-first began. I was returning to Paris after a visit to certain large aviation fields in the neighborhood, and got off at this junction for luncheon and a change of cars. Few French trains now carry restaurant wagons, and travelers, except on express trains, have to carry luncheon baskets or depend on station buffets.

I arrived at the junction at eleven o'clock, but I did not take the two o'clock Paris express, as I had planned. I stayed in the station all day and all evening watching the breath-taking procession of trains tearing northward to the fight, and the equally amazing procession of trains rolling southward and bearing the flotsam and jetsam of battle—wounded and dying men, despairing refugees, damaged guns, broken airplanes. French trains, including our own over there, move methodically in blocks called *marches*. They never have any traffic tie-ups, because all the trains move at exactly the same speed, and every train has its prescribed place in the *marche*, just so far ahead or behind the next train. It is an excellent system. But it seemed to me that day that the trains would certainly telescope one another, they came on and on so unceasingly and so close together.

The trains moving northward were laden with soldiers, horses, guns, airplanes, ammunition wagons, food, supplies of every conceivable description. Trainload after trainload of horses, eight to a car with four men, generally asleep on the hay in the middle space of the car. The horses, beautiful, tragic creatures, going to almost certain destruction wrung the heart to see. They gazed out at the flying landscape and the cheering station crowds with big, soft, uncomprehending eyes. How I wish we did not have to use horses in war. Of course the lives of men are far more valuable, but the men at least know why they fight and die.

Trainloads of men, so many that within an hour I had ceased to count them, rolled through that junction. Men from England, Frenchmen hurriedly recalled from leave in their southern homes. All ages. I saw French boys who must have been eighteen, but who looked younger by two years, and I saw men who might have been grandfathers. These older men do not often fight. They serve meals in the trenches and perform other non-combatant services. All France—all—is mobilized for some kind of service.

Sometimes these troop trains made brief stops at our station. Of course, there was a Red Cross canteen there, and I worked with the fine French women who were in charge of it, ladling hot coffee into mugs, and handing thick sandwiches to the crowding, hungry *poilus*. Some of the trains had their own kitchens, portable affairs on flat cars, and when the train stopped the men fairly boiled out of the carriages, pails and bowls in hand, to get the delicious soup prepared by the cooks. The Red Cross women supplemented the meal with sandwiches and coffee, at least when time permitted, which was not often. Those troop trains were on their way north with no unnecessary stops.

More often than not the trains did not stop. Once as a train was rolling through the station a soldier called to me asking for the newspaper I held in my hand. Of course I gave it to him, sprinting along the platform at a lively rate. The next time I saw a train coming I ran to the newsstand and bought three francs' worth of papers, about as many as I could carry, and had them ready for rapid distribution to the effusive and laughing soldiers.

But right in the middle of that exciting procession of trains came something that brought my heart to my throat. It was an immensely long train of all new cars, painted olive drab, with U. S. A. in white letters on the side. And the cars, dozens and dozens of them, were loaded with railroad building material. Portable tracks, switches, signals, exactly like the expensive and fascinating toy railroads which children delight in. Steel rails, wooden ties, machinery for laying them, flat cars, wheels, tools and nails, and last of all tiny little locomotives, two of them to a flat car, all American, going up to the front with the French and the English soldiers.

Right behind that train of cars came another, a shorter one, and this was full of brown-clad American engineers, going up to the front with the allied soldiers, to lay those tracks and operate that little narrow-gauge railroad under gun-fire. Our own sons.

That was not all. In the middle of the afternoon another train went northward, olive drab, with U. S. A. in white letters. This was a hospital train of entirely new cars, the finest and most complete I had ever seen. It was a palace on wheels, with every conceivable appliance for the comfort of wounded soldiers. There were kitchen cars, operating cars, X-ray compartments, cars with beds, cars with couches for the sitting cases. Cars for doctors and nurses as well as patients. Nothing I had seen, not even men going into the trenches, brought home to me so sharply the fact that we were in the war and were fully determined to hold our end up.

We could not have done it so well had we not, in the last fifty years, developed such extraordinary railroad builders and operators. The French had a railroad system adequate for peace-time uses, but when war came, and especially after the tide of Americans began to pour into the country, the system had to be enormously enlarged. It had to be planned and organized also, in order not to disturb unduly the life of the country. And it had to be done quickly.

It is not going beyond the permissible line to say that our railroad experts have worked out a wonderful system for the transportation of men and supplies. Several big seaports in the northwest now receive most of the men who in larger and larger units are being transported to France. One very large port in the southwest is the receiving station of most of the supplies sent over. A network of railroads, some of which we have double-tracked, convey these men and the supplies eastward and northward to their destinations. There is never any confusion of freight and passenger trains, because they do not start from the same ports, and most of the time they are not even on the same lines.

All through central France along this railroad system the Americans have taken over old towns and cities as bases for war work. Outside of the towns are great camps, with army bakeries, quartermasters' depots, hospitals, shops and factories. In one of these camps, near a railroad junction, is a supply station which is preparing to feed a million men at the front. At another camp I saw a distribution depot for medical and surgical supplies for the whole army. At both of these camps railroad building was going on at a lively rate, miles and miles of spurs and switches.

At a lovely old town which was once the stronghold of feudal barons, whose hoary old château rises over the place like a watch tower, I saw an immense factory for repairing locomotives and rolling stock. It was no flimsy wooden structure built for a few months, but an enormous mass of brick and concrete such as we build in Pittsburgh and Gary. I saw in the woods outside this town gangs of American foresters. I saw American sawmills. I saw logging trains manned by Americans.

I have seen American workmen making wagons, portable houses, trucks, locomotives. I have seen them building cold storage warehouses and ice-making plants. Building them substantially, as though we had moved to Europe to stay, as indeed we have until we put the war out of the world, together with the militarism that made it.

Do the Germans know it? Their leaders do, of course, but I doubt very much whether the mass of the people do. Working under guard in many of our camps in France are gangs of German prisoners. Watching several hundred of these men, in fierce green uniforms and shapeless boots, I asked the young officer who was my escort what they thought of the American activities.

"I was curious about that, too," he replied, "and I took pains to find out. Would you believe it, that most of the prisoners refuse to credit the fact that we are here at all? They say, 'Before we were taken prisoner our officers told us that we would see soldiers who would claim to be Americans, but they aren't. They are Canadians or English. The Americans can not get over here. Our kaiser has said so.'"

In another camp I asked the same question. What did the Germans think about us? They say, I was told, that they didn't mind building railroads in France. The kaiser would be glad to have them when he came. What will happen to the kaiser when the German people learn the truth?

# CHAPTER IV
## PIONEERS, OH, PIONEERS

THE man on sentry duty on that section of the huge unfinished wharf was in a bad humor. He was in a very bad humor. If a stray cat or dog had appeared on the wharf at that moment he would probably have kicked it. As it was a woman in the khaki-colored uniform of a war correspondent, the sentry contented himself with roaring a challenge that brought her up standing. Having produced her pass, he stood aside with a scowl, shouldered the rifle which had been pointed at her most menacingly, and made a gesture with his head which meant, "Well, then, move on."

But the correspondent—I was the correspondent—did not move on. I stopped and said, mildly: "You don't seem to be enjoying yourself to-day. What's the matter?"

"What's the matter?" he repeated furiously. "Every darn thing is the matter. What did I leave my business for, what did I leave my wife and kids for? Why, to come over here and fight the boche. And what am I doing? Roustabout work on a blasted line of docks, miles away from the front. Been here five months in this hole, working like a subway digger.

"Look at the town back there where we go for a bit of amusement when the day's over. Worse than any slum back home. Talk about the horrors of the trenches. I'd swap the mud we live in for any trench. Talk about Fritz's poison gas. When the wind's right the fumes from that picric acid factory up the river blow down and choke the lungs out of us."

"Do you get these spells often?" I asked. Whereupon he grinned a little and relaxed his scowl. I asked him where he lived and he named a thriving town in western Kansas. He had a real estate business in town, but his folks still lived on the big farm which his father had proved up on forty years ago. It was a fine place, yielding a big income, enough to keep the old people in comfort for the rest of their lives, and to support his young family while he was at the war.

I came from the prairies myself, and I could just see that farm and the old folks who had gone out to Kansas in their lusty youth to take up government land. They had built a sod house, turned up the tough prairie grass, plowed and sowed and cultivated under the burning sun, performed the terrible labor to get their first meager corn crops.

They had fought drought and grasshoppers, lived through blizzards and cyclones, endured poverty and privations untold. They were pioneers. Of such is the greatness and the virtue of our America.

I sat down on a nail keg and talked to that lonely, homesick, aggrieved soldier about the pioneers. From England first, and later from every other country in the world they had come, moved by the divine unrest of ambitious spirits, to the United States.

They had crossed the plains in rough wagons, daring weather, starvation and thirst, hostile Indians. They had leveled forests, they had built homes with no tools but axes and hand saws. They had farmed arid lands. They had lived in caves and dugouts. They had raised corn that some years they had been forced to burn for fuel because there was no market for it. But they lived, and won out, and built homes for their children.

And now, once more the Americans are pioneering. They are pioneering in France. They are building an army and doing it, as their fathers before them, from the ground up. "If you were not building these miles of docks and warehouses, if we didn't have hundreds of thousands of men constructing ice plants, storage warehouses, railroads, barracks, bakeries, hangars, hospitals, how would the men in the trenches get food and ammunition and clothes and medical supplies and everything else they have to have before they can win the war?" I put it to him straight, and he turned an uncomfortable pink.

"Of course, you are right," he said. "But we have to blow off once in a while. You see we didn't know anything about it before we came. We drew our numbers in the draft, and most of us were mighty glad of it. We had the time of our lives in training camp, and we thought we were going right into the big show.

"We thought the engineers would be right up at the front building railroads for the artillery. Instead of that we are kept down here, hundreds of miles from the fighting, doing the kind of hard labor some of us have money enough to hire done at home.

"Why, do you know," he continued, "that in——," naming a near-by engineering camp, where immense seaplane hangars were being built, "there is one company of two hundred and fifty men, every one a graduate of a university or a technical school? All of those men are in overalls, doing day labor."

I did know those men. I had seen them, or some of them, the day before at the noon hour smoking short pipes and cigarettes, sitting or sprawling on their backs beside the road. And a fine, husky, happy lot they were, too.

Nothing in their university careers ever did for them what this rough job of pioneering was doing.

There was one man there who had put in a magnificent water system in his home town. When he went to France the newspapers gave him a great send-off, described his work, and said that no doubt he would be called on to take charge of the water system in one of the large French cities. When I met him he was acting as water boy to a railroad tie carrying squad.

The engineers in this part of France publish a monthly magazine called *The Spiker*. They love to get hold of these newspapers notices and to publish them with comments. From a San Francisco paper they gleaned that "Willie ———, the cotillion leader of last season's younger set, leaves for France shortly with the Blankth Engineers to take charge, it is understood, of the construction of a telephone system contemplated by the government to facilitate the hauling of troops to the front."

The comment records that the erstwhile cotillion leader, Private ———, is now on the business end of a No. 2 shovel.

Well, what of it? The shovel work has to be done just as the prairie sod had to be turned. The men growl about it sometimes, but mostly they grin. They chalk "P. G." on the backs of their jumpers, the same letters appearing in white on the vivid green uniforms of the German captives at work in many camps.

They mean *Prisonnier de Guerre*, war prisoner, and when the weather is cold and rainy and letters from home are delayed, and spirits sink, you can hardly blame the men from feeling at times a little like prisoners. They had expected excitement and perhaps some glory, and hard work and isolation is their lot.

But what they are doing, tedious enough day by day, is in the aggregate splendid and invaluable to the success of our army. The like of it was never done before by any army in the world. When the Germans see it, as they will some day through their newspapers, they will be aghast at the hugeness of it.

They had sneered at the idea of the Americans sending a large army to France. How could they send an army? An army can't swim, nor can it fly, and the Americans had no ships. Even if they found ships and sent men enough, how could they feed, clothe and equip them? How could they keep up their supplies?

The Americans could and did perform all these miracles because they had in them the blood of pioneers, of men and women whom no difficulties could afright, no obstacles turn back. Our soldiers have proved themselves in countless army camps abroad to be worthy sons of the breed.

I remember one big aviation camp which was built in a few months out of short lengths of boards because the colonel and his staff couldn't get any better lumber. They were told that they couldn't buy any lumber at all, that there was none available in that part of France. But they did get it, and they built the camp. The men lived in tents during the coldest weeks of winter with icy winds blowing over the barren plain. All aviation camps are built on big plains.

In spite of the cold the men had no stoves furnished them. No doubt stoves were contemplated, but they did not reach the camp. But you can't freeze pioneers. Those boys just went to work and built stoves, built them out of mud, brick and stones, oil cans and biscuit tins and any other old junk they could find lying around. They made stovepipes out of condensed milk cans, and they kept warm.

I met and talked with half a dozen of those engineers who were caught in that German counter-drive near Cambrai in November, 1917. The men, it will be remembered, were engaged in peaceful labor behind the British front, linking up railroad communications and forwarding supplies needed by the English soldiers farther up the line. No one supposed that the engineers were in any danger, and the squads went out without any firearms.

But unexpectedly the Germans swept over the British lines and the American engineers suddenly found themselves in the middle of a battle. Some of them seized arms from fallen men and sailed in to the fight like seasoned soldiers. Others had no chance to get hold of guns, but did they retreat? Not so that you could notice it. They went for the Germans with their picks and shovels, and what they did to them was epic. In describing their work the British general in command said it was futile to bestow praise on the Americans. What they did was beyond praise.

When I met these men they were just finishing up a piece of construction work at a camp in central France. It was not an especially interesting work, just day labor. But when the big push began in March these men, being free to move, were sent up to the front to build more railroads.

"Aren't they the lucky stiffs?" groaned a man in another labor group. "But our turn will come, I'll bet you."

The lucky stiffs agreed that they were lucky, but they refrained out of politeness from saying too much about it. Of course, every man hopes to get up into the big show. But the work behind the lines has to be done.

That is the spirit of the army, except on occasions when the men have to blow off steam.

Bidding the lucky ones good-by, I expressed a hope that they would be allowed to carry weapons when next they went near a fighting line. They said that they were going to carry side arms, but one man said:

"What's the matter with a good sharp pick when you meet up with Heinie? He knows what a gun will do to him and he is game. But a Yankee guy with a pick has got him backed off of the map. Jim here killed two and chased two more with nothing in his hands but a shovel. I had a pick and I was better off than him."

Which was his modest way of telling that he and his pick had accounted for three German soldiers armed with rifles and bayonets. Thus had his grandfather fought wolves in some western forest, or killed rattlers in prairie grass. Pioneers! You can't beat them.

# CHAPTER V
## WE FINISH WHAT CÆSAR BEGAN

A STANDARD joke, used with several variations in French music-halls, is to the effect that "the English only leased their trenches for three years, but the Americans have bought theirs." This witticism is a tribute to the amount of solid preparation the Americans have made and are making and to the marvelous feats of engineering which are progressing rapidly from southern and western France clear up to the battle lines.

We own, temporarily at least, seven miles of docks and wharves in one great seaport alone. Most of these we have built, and the work is still going on. For forty miles around this seaport the sound of hammer and ax rings day after day as one after another camp and cantonment is established. Some of these camps are really small cities. In one, for example, a hospital camp will house thirty-five thousand people. Provision for twenty thousand beds is being made. It will be, when completed, the largest hospital in the world.

A few months ago that hospital site was a barren waste of prairie. As for water, there was one solitary well. Sewers there were none, and, of course, no streets. Now there is a model drainage and sewer system. There are a dozen miles of paved streets. There is a good water supply, electric lights and telephones. When I visited this camp some fifty hospital buildings were wholly or partially completed, and since then many more must have been built.

Most of the materials used in this vast piece of construction came overseas from the United States, but no small amount of lumber was purchased in France. Now France is very short of lumber and sells as little of it as she can. I asked the colonel in command of the work where he got his building material, and he replied with a broad smile: "Well, I really stole it. I had to have the lumber, so when I found out where it was, I went over there and just insisted. You see," he added, "over here no excuses are ever accepted from anybody. You simply have to make good on any job they assign you to. If for any reason you don't make good, you get sent home."

If we could make up our minds to apply this inexorable method to some of the people who are doing war work on this side of the water we might get better results. At one of the camps in the neighborhood of this same seaport in France they are building a naval aviation station. When it is complete there will be provision for one thousand to fifteen hundred giant seaplanes, great white birds that can sail three days out to sea, that will possess power to sink more submarines than any armed vessels. The submarine is visible from the air at a much greater depth than it is from a ship's deck, and the seaplanes will carry plenty of deadly depth bombs. Moreover, they will fly safely. The submarine can not fight back at them.

When this camp is completed and equipped—don't forget that it has to be equipped—those planes will do more than convoy vessels into the harbor, they will be used to train flyers for a dozen other ports into which our ships and our allies' ships now steal precariously. There were no seaplanes there when I saw the place. The hangars were soon to be ready, though, and so were the big repair shops, the bunkhouses for the men, the ammunition warehouses, and all the other necessary buildings. There is absolutely no inefficiency over there.

The man who is in charge of most of the mammoth undertaking in and around this seaport now bears the title of colonel. Before he entered his country's service for the duration of the war he was known as one of the greatest engineers in America. His largest feat was the canal which connects Lake Washington with Puget Sound. To build this canal, which flows through the heart of the city of Seattle, the waters of the big lake, which is nearly twenty miles long, had to be lowered nine feet. To a man who could do that without difficulty or serious accident the work undertaken by our army forces in France was a mere matter of taking one step after another. The first step was getting men, and there was no difficulty about that. The draft furnished the men, or at least the mass of them. Voluntary enlistment furnished experts in various lines. And splendid men they are, those American builders in France. Of one regiment of engineers working for the most part as day laborers there fully sixty per cent. are college graduates.

This seaport lies at one end of a vast railroad system which is carrying our men and all the army supplies from the ocean to the fighting front. It is a good harbor and a famous one from the time of the Romans and even further back than the Romans. But for present-day war needs it is not good enough. It has sandbars and shallows, so one of the engineering feats our men are doing is the deepening of that harbor to admit the largest ships.

Another feat is the enlarging of docking facilities so that supplies for an army of three or four million men may be quickly unloaded. Another still is the building of a five-track spur from the docks to the main line of railroad. It would take many chapters to describe adequately all the construction work that is being done in and around this one city in southern France.

Perhaps it is nobody's fault on this side of the Atlantic that a great deal of the work has been delayed for lack of tools and machinery, but delayed it has been. For example, pile drivers that were urgently needed came slowly, and when they came were found to be relics of the past and practically useless. Locomotives of the vintage of 1868 were grudgingly furnished, and important work was held up while they were put into shape. Steam shovels came a piece at a time. But no matter. The engineers hustled while they waited and built with what material they had on hand.

If Germany has spies in those camps, and if they have contrived to make reports on what is happening there, the knowledge will bring no comfort to Emperor William and his junkers. The Potsdam fire department which was to dispose of all the army that the United States could send to Europe will be assigned to a simpler task. The mere personnel of that working force of engineers in southern France is enough to make the Germans turn pale.

The man in charge of repairs and equipment of naval aviation, with headquarters in this southern port made a fortune in the automobile manufacturing business and just before the war he retired from business. He is still young, but he had all the money he needed and he wanted to enjoy life in other ways than business. Now he draws the pay of a lieutenant-commander in the navy and devotes what time he has free from his duties to inducing other successful business men to enter army service. This man was on the boat with me coming home from France. He was going back to get three thousand more expert mechanics, and incidentally to persuade one of the biggest millionaire railroad men in the country to put on a uniform.

A captain of engineers who is bossing part of the work of building warehouses was drawing a salary of fifteen thousand a year in the contracting business in New York. Working under him in overalls are master mechanics, machinists, bridge carpenters, skilled men of many trades. They may seem to be wasted on these laboring jobs, but the work has to be done, and there are not enough men of lesser skill to go around. Later these men will be found and the skilled ones will be overseers.

To this end the world is being scoured for laborers. We have Chinese coolies working for us, Japanese, Spaniards, Dutch, Scandinavians. In one camp I saw a large detachment of Africans from Algeria, Mohammedans. They were under the command of French non-commissioned officers, men who had spent years in North Africa and know the language. The colonel in command took me to their quarters and into the cook house, where the noon meal was in preparation. A giant African in a white cotton robe and turban, the sweat running in streams down his face, was making soup in a great copper caldron. Other men, similarly attired and equally hot, were slicing vegetables, cutting bread into big chunks, opening cans of tomatoes and pouring the contents into the stew which formed the basis of the meal.

"I can't get used to this job of mine," said the colonel. "A year ago I filled a little army department job at home and was getting old and fat. Now I am responsible for a regiment of engineers and nine hundred workmen, most of whom can't speak a word of English.

"These Africans, for instance. I have to leave them to their French sergeants, and look how they manage them." I looked. The squad that was laying bricks for a drain outside the cook house had apparently committed a slight breach of discipline, for the lithe little French sergeant in charge was administering punishment. He was bounding around in a series of catlike jumps, at each jump landing an amazing kick on exactly the same portion of each man's anatomy. He never said a word, he just leaped and kicked.

"Now, what ought I to do about that?" demanded the colonel. "It's against every rule and procedure of the American army."

I suggested that the American army was in process of upheaval in a good many directions, and he agreed with me.

I ought not to leave the Africans without paying a tribute to the American negroes who by thousands are helping to build camps and railroads and docks in southern France. And in many other parts of France as well. They are doing splendid work and behaving wonderfully well. France is bewildering to these men, and one of the most bewildering things is the fact that it has a dark-skinned population which does not speak United States. It is enough to rattle any good-natured black man from a Louisiana rice field to speak to a brother laborer and have him answer back in French or Arabic.

"Go 'way with tha' talk," he exclaims. "You ain't no real colored man nohow. Cain't speak your own language."

But if the colored American is short on language in a foreign land he is all there when it comes to imagination. Some of the men from the far South are illiterate, but the majority can read and write, and according to the regimental censors some of the letters they write home to the folks must keep Georgia and Mississippi neighborhoods keyed up to the boiling point of excitement. Hundreds of miles removed from the fighting lines does not prevent the letters from dripping gore.

"Just back from a hard day in the trenches," writes a man whose job is working on a slag heap. "I tell you we done some bloody work. I tell you. We killed a hundred Germans in one trench and cut um up like sausage meat. I cut a officer's head clean off with my bayonet. I cuts Germans ears off when I kills um. I got a whole string of ears in my bunkhouse. Write soon, 'cause I might get hit with one of them big guns and killed."

These lurid recitals emanate from the gentlest and most childlike of all our enlisted forces. They sit around evenings in the Y. M. C. A. huts reserved for them, eat candy, look at illustrated papers and sing their plantation and campmeeting songs in voices sweet and lonely. The French children creep up to the doors and windows of the huts to look and listen in wonder. Of all the queer and fascinating Americans in their land the colored men are the queerest and most fascinating. If it were not for the children and their shy friendliness I don't know what the colored fellow would do, for he is very, very far from home.

---

# CHAPTER VI
# GOING TO SCHOOL IN THE ARMY

RIDICULING and belittling the American army in France is no longer the great indoor sport of the German government. It was the last one the government has left and until lately it was played desperately with the view of diverting the minds of the people, and keeping hope alive in their sinking hearts.

The German newspapers, of course, are rigidly censored. Not a word of war news is ever published except that which emanates from headquarters. Nevertheless, the German people, who are not fools, now know full well that the kaiser's war promises are not being fulfilled. He promised in the beginning that their victorious troops would be home by Christmas of 1914. They know now that Christmas, 1918, will see the world still at war.

The kaiser promised his people Verdun, but he could not deliver Verdun. He promised them the annihilation of the British army before this year's summer. But the British army still fights on and even the German newspapers dare not claim that the British show signs of weakness or surrender.

The German people were promised, above all, that their commander-in-chief would end the war victoriously before the Americans could raise and transport overseas any army worthy of the name. This supreme promise the government, until Pershing annihilated the St. Michiel salient, tried to make the people believe was being kept. Because they knew that unless the war was won before the Americans come in in great numbers, it never could be won.

Secretary of War Baker, quoting from the semi-official *Norddeutsche Allgemeine Zeitung* of Berlin, gives a sample of the sedative stuff with which the German authorities kept the people's nerves quiet. Admitting that a country of one hundred million population might conceivably raise an army of one million five hundred thousand men, the article goes to great pains to prove that such an army will never cross the seas. "The American political situation" is such that the greater part of the army will have to be kept at home. At best only four to five hundred thousand men can be put into the European battle-field.

"There is an American army in France," concedes the article, with an air of being quite candid on the subject, "but it consists entirely of woodcutters, railroad men and doctors, except two or three divisions whose precious lives are being spared in quiet places far behind the front."

When I read those words I laughed. Because I have been in a good many of those quiet places behind the front, and I know that what was being done there was not coddling American soldiers, nor yet keeping them safe from battle. What was and is being done there is making them one hundred per cent. efficient fighters. Not mass fighters alone, not men who at the word of command go forward to be mown down by machine-gun fire. But individual fighters, men who can move together in a mass, yes, but men who also know how to fight alone, who have initiative, resourcefulness, responsibility. Men who know every trick in the game.

While we were building ships; while we were drafting and drilling men over here; while the despised woodcutters and railroad men and the vigorous young engineers were laying the basis for a long war if necessary, but a clean victory in the end, our soldiers, waiting in scores of camps to take their places in the lines, were being given an intensive training, which I think would astonish even the war-efficient Germans.

We have also special schools for officers, and they are still in full blast, and will be continued as long as they are needed. Our supply of officers will never run short, for the schools will continue to turn them out. The schools give the superior enlisted men a chance to earn commissions. Officers in every regiment are on a constant watch for men who show signs of leadership and military intelligence. Such men are officer material, and on the recommendation of their superiors they are sent to one or another of the schools which have been established over there.

When our men go to France from the cantonments here their training is by no means complete. They have been licked into soldier shape, they are in good physical and mental condition, they have learned to march, to drill, and to shoot. They can use the bayonet, they know something about artillery, about grenades and bombs. But they still have much to learn. They begin to learn soon after they arrive in France. They learn in camps and schools, but the German government doesn't tell its people about that.

It was a cold, drizzly day in March that I visited a school where infantry, artillery, sanitary and gas lore was being instilled into the intelligence of nearly two thousand hot-blooded young Americans. Some of them were being trained for non-commissioned officers who would be in direct command of squads of soldiers in battle. There were also large classes for lieutenants and captains of infantry, artillery, engineering and aviation.

I can not in one chapter or in two give anything more than an outline of the courses studied. The schedules announcing the classes lie on my desk as I write. They cover eighteen closely typewritten pages.

Take a class of enlisted infantry men who were expected to command squads. These are some of the things they did in school the week of March 4 to March 9, 1918: On Monday and Tuesday they had inspection and drill from 7:50 to 8:45. From 9 until 11:45 they had instruction in musketry, grenade and bayonet work. They went to their noon dinner, and from 1:15 to 4:30 they had more of the same kind of drill.

They repeated this during the rest of the week, and on Wednesday they had besides a lecture on some theoretical problem of their work by a veteran colonel, a West Point man. They also studied a map problem, and in the evening they saw in the engineers' school a night demonstration of wiring in the field. They finished on Saturday afternoon with a "tactical walk." Quite a busy week.

It was just as busy with the class in automatic weapons. On Monday they had close order drill, barrage drill, a lecture on direct fire, another on indirect fire, practise in range firing and the use of range finders. Finally they had an hour's pistol practise.

They had a great deal of artillery target practise that week, also a lecture on trench routing, a conference on indirect fire tables, whatever they may be, and two days' hard work in the gas school. You can not, you know, just pick up a gas mask, put it on and successfully fight. You have to learn how. I tried on a gas mask and couldn't breath in it five minutes. So the soldiers have to learn how to wear their masks, and a great deal besides before they can safely face a gas attack.

They hear lectures on how gas is used, preparation for the attacks, on the mechanics of the box respirator used by our army, and on the effects of gas. They learn the history of gas warfare and the German orders and reports concerning it. They learn what to do during and after an attack. They drill in actual gas chambers.

The officers in this school had much more technical work. A tactical course for field officers interested me greatly. The men studied the technique of grenade, trench mortar and one pound cannon firing. Trench fighting, when I visited the school, was being vigorously studied, and I heard part of an intensely interesting lecture on "The Attack in Trench Warfare," from a lieutenant-colonel of the British army who had led many such attacks himself since 1915.

It seems odd to hear of seminars in war wisdom, but they have them there, officers who had experienced trench fighting sitting around a table and discussing nice questions of tactics, just as a short time ago some of them were sitting around university tables and discussing political economy or English literature.

They had a course for signal men which was very valuable. Field telegraphs and telephones play an exciting part in modern battles, and the students in this course devoted much time to buzzer telegraph work. They learned how to string field telephones, and to use them. They had lectures on ciphers and signals, endless and intricate. They learned to read maps.

In the aero school they were training aerial photographers and teaching them how to interpret photographs taken in the skies. The flyers were being taught to signal troops from above and to read army signals thousands of feet below. What the soldiers on the ground seemed to be doing was spreading freshly washed towels and sheets on the grass, but what they were really doing, it appeared, was asking questions of the aviators about the enemy's maneuvers.

A little later I visited another army school, or rather an army college, for there line and staff officers of superior rank were under instruction. Our army authorities do not intend to repeat the mistakes of the Civil War in regard to superior officers. It has been said that it took only a year to teach the rank and file of our men to fight, but that we fought for two years to train lieutenants and captains, and three years to train generals. The war was ended in one more year.

This war college in France, where some great general may now be in training, perhaps for the highest command of all, is located in a medieval town which must have seen a lot of fighting in the distant past. Its stout city walls still stand, and it is plain that a long battle would have to be fought before the besieging army reached the walls. The town stands on a rocky height little accessible in the old days. Below stretches a level plain where all the enemy's movements would have been visible for miles.

It is an appropriate place in which to train future American generals, for this war is being fought, not only with all modern weapons, but with many of the weapons of the past. One can easily fancy the ghosts of the great Charlemagne, Godfrey of Bouillon, Richard Lion Heart, Sir John Chandos, hovering in the shadows of the classrooms, and listening delightedly to familiar things, talk of liquid fire, hand grenades, storming positions with bayonets and long knives.

But the ghostly warriors would hear other talk, and when final examination time came, I imagine that they might thank their stars that they were safely dead, for this war makes demands on the intelligence of commanding officers that the middle ages wotted nothing of.

I took a brief survey of one examination paper in which it was put up to a commander to move several divisions of men from one district in France to the fighting front. He had a railroad map of France before him and he was required to state at length and in detail exactly how and when and where he would entrain his one hundred and twenty-five thousand men; when and where he would stop each unit for meals; what he would do with his men when they left the railroad; what villages and towns he would occupy; where he would billet the soldiers; how and with what he would feed and supply them; how he would move supplies. It made my head swim, but it also made my heart swell with proud confidence in our army.

Efficiency! There is only one real and permanent efficiency. It is not possible to achieve it under a slave system. It can only be achieved by freemen, willing to follow their chosen leaders into the valley of the shadow of death if that is the road through which more freedom, freedom of all the world, is to be gained.

# CHAPTER VII
# OUR BOYS DISCOVER THE PAST

"Voilà," said the old French general who sat opposite me in the Bordeaux express, "behold the prettiest sight in France." He pointed through the open door of the compartment to two soldiers who were standing in the corridor smoking their after-luncheon cigarettes.

One of the soldiers wore a horizon blue uniform, a little worn and stained with hard usage, although the boy was barely twenty-one. The other soldier's uniform was brand new O. D. cloth, made in America. The two stood beside the window, their arms entwined, looking at the lovely valley of the Loire and teaching each other their respective languages.

"Sammee," said the French soldier, "how you say '*donnes moi une allumette*'?"

"You say 'gimme a match.' But listen here, Gaston, cut out the Sammie. Forget it."

"What you mean 'forget it,' Sammee?" persisted the *poilu*, accepting the match. The lesson went on, and I agreed with the old general that the sight of French and American youths associating on affectionate terms and learning each other's familiar argot was indeed agreeable.

One of the stock arguments of the pacifists in trying to make war out an unmixed evil is that it sets back education. I am sure that many American mothers have had misgivings on this point, and have deplored the necessity of interrupting their sons' college life. But I want to assure them that their sons are learning more in France than any college could have taught them. They are learning French, for one thing, at least all the enterprising ones are. Not the foolish, academic sort of thing they study in high school and college, the object being to read Molière and the classics, but the living language.

A striking illustration of the difference in the two methods was afforded me during a trip into the war zone. In the party was one of our intelligence officers and a French woman writer of unusually broad education. The American officer spoke very little French, the woman writer spoke only a few broken sentences of English, and they had to be constantly interpreted to each other. One day, in the course of the conversation, it transpired that the officer before joining the colors had been a high-school professor of French, and that the woman had for five years drawn a good salary as a teacher of English.

The American soldier in a few months can, if he wants to, gets a practical knowledge of the French language that will be a business asset to him all his life. Most of the soldiers appreciate this, and the free classes offered in all the Y. M. C. A. centers are well attended. They learn in the classes, and they learn even more by association with French soldiers and civilians.

My soldier son knew not a word of the language when he enlisted, but when I saw him in France he was using it fairly well. I congratulated him on his new acquisition, and he laughed and said: "There's an awfully pretty girl in a café the fellows up our way patronize, and she doesn't know any English."

It is not only the French language that our soldiers are learning, but French history as well. The part of central France occupied by our army is a storied treasure house of history. No part of France is more French. It abounds in castles, châteaux, museums, pointed towers, dungeon cells and torture chambers, ancient churches and crumbling city walls. Even the farms, centuries old, some of them, show the remains of past defenses.

To our boys, fresh from the new prairies of Iowa and Dakota, or the still virgin forests of Oregon and Washington, this past they are surrounded by is the most romantic and wonderful thing that ever came into their lives. They can hardly believe it is real.

Even to those soldiers who come from the older sections of the United States the sight is thrilling. In the gardens of the Luxembourg Palace, in Paris, built by Henry of Navarre for his second wife, Marie de Medici, stands a stately marble fountain, moss-grown and mellow with time. The date cut in the marble is 1620.

I had this pointed out to me by a soldier from Massachusetts. "Think of it," he exclaimed, "the very year when our oldest aristocracy, the Pilgrim fathers, were cutting down trees for their first log huts and their rude stockades, these French people were making beautiful things like that fountain."

Long before that they were building beautiful things. Down in the southernmost part of our territory in France stand the ruins of a magnificent castle, the one where Edward the Black Prince took refuge when he was being pursued by that French king with whom he was contesting the crown of France in thirteen hundred and something. With two young naval officers I explored the place one warm spring day, and we were actually awed by the achievement of those builders of olden days.

The castle was not only strong, it was noble and fine in all its masses. "It makes you proud of your Norman ancestors," said one of the American officers, a Virginian.

You can not go into one of the old Gothic churches or cathedrals on Sunday or week-days without meeting American soldiers, caps in hand, gazing silently at twelfth century Madonnas and saints, or tombs of medieval bishops. The miracle and charm of Gothic architecture is not all that draws our boys to the old churches. The sense of time and antiquity possesses them. It is something entirely new and wonderful to them to realize that the world went on, that people lived and loved and thought about themselves as modern and up-to-date centuries before Columbus discovered America.

In a certain French city, where I made friends with many American soldiers, a group of university professors are making it their business to escort our soldiers over the place, giving them historical talks. This is a very old city, one in which the Romans had a considerable occupation. The ruins of an immense circus built by them still stands in the midst of modern houses and shops. Its masonry is so solid that a ton of dynamite would be required to dislodge it.

At the time of the French revolution it was practically intact, but its use as a fortress and the pounding of cannon against it turned it into the picturesque ruin it is to-day. Our soldiers are exploring that old circus and realizing the grandeur that was Rome more keenly than if they were cramming Latin back home.

"You positively mustn't miss the mummies," I was told by my soldier friends in this same city. So one day I went with two boys to see the mummies. There is an ancient church built, centuries ago, outside the city walls, when the town was just beginning to outgrow its walls. The excuse for the walls had not disappeared, however, and local wars and forays among the feudal gentry beat hard on that church. Several times during the years the church was burned to the ground, but it was always rebuilt according to its original plans.

The last time it was rebuilt was about a hundred and fifty years ago, and it was when the excavations were being made that the famous mummies were discovered. They were dug up out of one of the oldest corners of the churchyard and must have passed from life in the fourteenth or the fifteenth century. Something in the chalky nature of the soil preserved them from disintegration, and they remain still rather disagreeable and grewsome likenesses of their original selves.

To see them we descended a flight of worn stone steps into the inky darkness of a crypt. An old, old crone of a woman, herself half a mummy, led the way, a sort of a dark lantern in her hand. She has told the story of the mummies several times a day for so many years that she could probably recite it without troubling herself to wake out of a nap. She can even recite it in a jargon which remotely resembles English.

The mummies, about twenty of them, are hung up like so many old clothes, around the walls of the crypt. Some are mere parchment shells of bodies, others retain rags of clothing, and even rings. The old, old crone turned her lantern on the mummies, one by one. Here was a priest, she said, you could tell by his soutaine. Here was a woman who had died in childbirth, her tiny baby buried with her. Here was a whole family, mother and four children, who had died of poison, perhaps mushrooms. This man was hanged. You could tell—"Ugh! Let's look at the next one, *ma mère*," we implored. The next one was worse, a cataleptic, buried alive.

"What in the world makes you want to look at such things?" I asked when we emerged, in time to meet another group of soldiers bent on the same errand.

"Why," they said, "don't you think it is terribly interesting to look at people who actually lived five hundred years ago? Those mummies are worth a franc any day."

Two Sundays before I left France I spent the afternoon in the Hotel des Invalides, where Napoleon lies in his granite tomb, now completely buried in sandbags. In spite of that fact, however, the chapel was filled with American soldiers gazing raptly at the tomb they could not see, but which they knew held the ashes of the great conqueror.

More soldiers were in the large courtyard, now a museum of captured Germans guns, cannon, "minnies" and shattered airplanes. There are the burned and charred skeletons of several Zeppelins, and in the very center of the collection, as if its captor, the remains, nearly intact, of Guynemer's favorite fighting plane, his "Old Charles" which brought so many German flyers to earth. This plane, white, with a scarlet symbolic bird in flight painted on its body, is decorated like a shrine, with a constantly renewed tribute of fresh flowers.

The American boys who wandered through the courtyard and long galleries of the Invalides that day were on their way to the front, and were spending every precious minute of their stay in Paris storing up impressions. I watched them studying with intent faces the marvelous collection of armor, some of it restoration work, but most of it the actual harness of kings and knights of old. Soldiers of all the ages, Greek, Roman, Gaul, Frenchmen of the age of chivalry, are represented in the collection. The whole history of warfare.

"When they are giving us tin hats why didn't they give us things like these?" sagely remarked one soldier. "These protect the eyes."

"But, gee!" exclaimed another, pausing in front of a "tin hat" the size of a garbage bucket and several times as heavy, "wouldn't you like to catch a Hun with one of them things on?"

Where the American soldiers lingered longest that day was in the gallery sacred to the relics of Napoleon. His camp bed is there, and they exclaimed at the smallness of the great soldier. There were also his camp chair, his writing table and books, scores of personal belongings, uniforms and decorations. The walls are covered with paintings of his battles and the stirring events of his life.

You'll never get those soldiers to agree that war sets education back. Our soldiers are learning at first-hand in France what they would never have learned so well at home, the great, big thing we are fighting for in this war, what in all ages the flower of manhood have fought and died for—better life, and more freedom for the generations next to come.

# CHAPTER VIII
# THE MAN WITHOUT A COUNTRY

THERE is one thing our soldier sons are learning in France that is more valuable than the French language or history or any mere knowledge acquisition. Our men are learning the true meaning of nationalism, love of country and the flag.

Of late years we have had in the United States such a deluge of talk about "internationalism" that our young men had almost reached the point of being ashamed to feel patriotism. An insidious propaganda of pacifism, beginning in elementary schools all over the country, had undermined the old American pride in the flag. The children went through the motions of saluting the flag, true, but in too many schoolrooms the poisonous suggestion was given them that it was much nobler to love all flags and all countries equally with their own.

A young Jewish soldier from the east side of New York told me that, when he learned that he had been drafted, he actually contemplated suicide. It seemed to him a crime for him to become a soldier. His parents had fled from Russia to escape death at the hands of soldiers, but that was not why he was opposed to all war. It was because in his school, and afterward in the city college, he had imbibed what is miscalled internationalism.

"I went to training camp because I was afraid to resist," said this young man. "I stayed and I worked hard because I liked it, liked my officers, and because, being assigned to the aviation service as a ground man, I knew I would not be obliged to kill Germans. I still believed that it was my duty to be international at heart."

And then he told me how the conviction came to him that men can not love all countries unless they love their own first and best. "You see that work gang over there," he said. "Those fellows are Russians. They are part of the Russian division that was sent to fight in France two or three years ago. You remember what a fine impression they made then. Well, after the revolution in Russia, or rather after the Bolshevist soldiers began running away from the fight, murdering their officers and clamoring for a separate peace, there was the question what to do with the Russian regiments in France.

"Some of the Russians it was impossible to trust. Some, at least, I don't know how many, were bitten with the German propaganda. They did what they could to demoralize the French soldiers. Nobody knew but that they might betray the allies in the middle of a battle. The upshot of the whole thing was that they sent the Russian troops back from the front, and now they work in labor gangs. They don't want to go back to their own country. Things are too bad there.

"Among our flyers was a young lieutenant who was born a Russian. Not a Jew, a Russian. He was finishing his training in this camp. It was partly the monotony and the lack of work that made him melancholy. You know we haven't enough practise planes and the flying men are idle half the time. But mainly it was the sight of those Russian laborers that got on his nerves. He used sometimes to talk to them, and they were pathetically glad to have him, because nobody else spoke their language and they were lonesome.

"He said to me once: 'When those poor devils landed in France the houses were decked with flags to greet them. The streets were full of cheering crowds and children threw flowers in their path. Now nobody trusts them to fight. They are outcasts. They have no country, and no country wants to adopt them.' I tried to tell him that he was wrong, that the allies wanted to help Russia to get back, but it was no good.

"By and by this man took it into his head that he was distrusted because he had been born a Russian. It wasn't true. But he thought it was. He said so. One day he went up in an altitude test with an observer. He was acting as pilot, but the machine had a double control and the man with him was a cool and capable flyer. Otherwise the thing might have been even worse than it was. For when they were six thousand feet up and still climbing, the Russian suddenly unbuckled the belt that secured him in his seat, and before the observer could even guess what he was about to do, he stepped over the side of the machine into space.

"That settled me. I said to myself that I would rather be dead than be a man without a country. That's what that poor fellow figured that he was, and all other Russians. But I'm not a Russian, nor an internationalist, nor anything else but a one hundred per cent. American, and if they want me to kill boches, I'm ready to begin any minute."

A man without a country. Is there any sentence in the language, any combination of words more dreadful? Yet what the German propagandists, which is the real name of many of the pacifists and "internationalists," have been trying to do to American youth is to take their country away from them. They nearly succeeded, and the proof of that was the three years of indifference we loitered through before we woke up to the fact that this war was ours, as well as England's, France's and Belgium's.

We failed to realize that our country was in immediate peril, because we had almost forgotten that we had a country. Are we all awake to the fact yet? No, because, if we were, there would not be left anywhere from the Atlantic Ocean to the Pacific one single disloyal citizen, one single copperhead or so-called internationalist. No community would tolerate them. There would be no corner where they could hide.

Some of the Socialist party leaders are beginning to see a great light on the subject of loyalty to the government, and are advocating a new policy toward the war. Their last party platform read like one of Trotzky's messages to the Petrograd Soviet, but now even the late Socialist candidate for mayor of New York, who appealed for the pacifist vote, and got it, is beginning to talk about revising the platform.

Unless it is revised, the Socialists are going to lose their adherents at present serving in France. The Jewish boys who, a little over a year ago, were orating from soap boxes against the draft and against what they called "this profiteers' war," are among the hottest young patriots and keenest fighters in the American army.

I saw some of those boys at Camp Upton last autumn. I saw one who was sitting in a corner blubbering like a small child because he was being sent to Spartanburg. He was being transferred because he was continually begging to be allowed to go home. His captain told me that the only thing to do with him was to send him so far away from New York that week-end visits home would be impossible.

I saw other Jewish boys who were unwilling soldiers then, but every one I saw in France was enthusiastic about his work, and as little of an internationalist as the young man in the aviation camp. The Jewish soldier has made good. I was told so by many officers, and I saw it for myself.

Our soldiers have not been taught to hate the Germans, and I don't think they do hate them. It is certain that the French people with whom our men associate do not. But they scorn and loathe the Hindenburg method of making war, and this attitude our men share. They regard the Germans with horror rather than hatred, and so must all Americans who even faintly realize what is going on every day and hour in the invaded districts of Belgium and France.

Our soldiers, many of them, have seen this terrible thing, and it has made their blood run hot in their arteries, it has set their jaws hard, and caused their eyes to blaze. What theories they have ever had about internationalism have been dissipated by the facts with which they are faced.

The submarine war has come home to our men, sometimes as a bitter personal experience.

In a Y. M. C. A. canteen I came upon a young corporal who had found a seat behind the piano, and he was sitting there weeping his heart out over a letter from home, a letter telling him how his brother had died when the Germans torpedoed the *Tuscania*. I sat down beside this soldier. He seemed to need somebody, and I was the only woman near. In a few minutes he was himself again, outwardly at least, and he read me the letter.

It was from his sister, because, she said, mother was taking it very hard and could not write yet. When the ship went down brother managed to get on a raft which was very much overcrowded. There were so many men on the raft that the brother's chum, who was in bad shape with a broken leg, was pushed off into the water.

Brother was a good swimmer and he managed to rescue his chum and to get him back on the raft. But while he was in the water two more men, half drowned and desperate, had climbed aboard, and the raft was now several inches under seas. So this heroic young American soldier, unwilling to jeopardize his comrades' life, gave up his own.

"Tell my mother and the family that I am sorry I didn't have a chance to fight for America," he said, and sank into the black and icy ocean.

"Well, I can fight," said the soldier who read me that letter. "And every time I am allowed to go over the top I shall remember how they killed my kid brother in the dark."

American men are accustomed from their childhood to see women treated with respect and children with tenderness. They see with horror-stricken eyes the women and children refugees from the war invaded districts flying before a foe that knows no pity, that treats combatant and non-combatant with equal cruelty and wrath.

I have told of a Sunday I spent in a railroad station in the first days of the great spring offensive, and of the southward bound trains bearing the wounded and the homeless. With me on that platform were several American soldiers, two or three members of the military police. They were there primarily to look after our soldiers passing up and down the line, but they worked hard to help the stricken refugees, hundreds of whom were fed and ministered to that day by the French Red Cross.

They were mostly women and children and old men, and their plight was pitiful. This was the second time that they had fled before the German hordes. Last November, after the "victorious retreat," they had crept back to their ruined and desolated villages and farms, and with the aid of their government and the American societies for French reconstruction had begun life again.

In their shells of houses and in their shattered little farms they gladly took up the work of gaining a little bread. Then, without any warning, the awful flood of war swept over them again.

They fled, half clad, never pausing to collect their poor belongings. Without the blessed help of the Red Cross they would have died of starvation on the road. Everything they ever had was gone. They stumbled off the trains, dazed, with white blank faces and staring empty eyes.

I saw those American soldiers carrying old women and little children into the Red Cross canteen, feeding them, ministering to them, all the time muttering curses on the fiends who had brought them to this bitter pass.

"Oh, we have work to do over here," one of these men said to me. "God help the kaiser when we get fairly into this war." And then he exclaimed: "Are there really any pacifists left in America? If there are I wish they could see what we have seen to-day."

I wish so, too. I wish I could show the theorists, the "internationalists," what I saw of those French refugees, the poor, despoiled working people and farmers who fled, as the hordes of old fled before Attila, another scourge of God, but one not less tigerish or void of soul.

# CHAPTER IX
# OUR FOREIGN LEGION

"DO THEY really call you Sammies?" I asked one of the first soldiers I met in France.

"They call us the foreign legion," he laughed. "I don't blame them, either. They expected American soldiers to be American, and we handed them an army made up of forty different nationalities. Come to think of it, that is America."

"I never realized it before," joined in a young sergeant sitting near. "My family has lived in Massachusetts for nearly three hundred years, and I always thought of myself and others like me as the only real Americans. The Italians, Greeks, Russians, and even the Irish, seemed to me to be grafted stock. But I am in charge of a bunch of fellows, not one of whom was born in the U. S. A., and I would back them as straight Americans against any man in the 'Descendants of John and Priscilla Alden' society.

"I've got two Czechs who ran away from their native land to avoid army service in Austria. That was five years before we got into the war, before there was a war. These boys hated army life and wouldn't stay in a country that had compulsory military service. But along comes a chance to fight for the U. S. A. and these same fellows just pant for it."

The first soldier spoke again. "But what do you think of a Russian who ran away from Russia during the war, and yet wanted to join the American army? By the way, he wants to meet you. May I introduce him?"

"Yes, indeed," I replied, whereupon the youth stood up and called out: "Oh, Trotzky! Come on over, Trotzky!" And the Russian soldier thus libeled came rather diffidently from an adjoining room. We were sitting before an open fire in a Y. M. C. A. headquarters.

"Trotzky," whose other name was Jeff Bramfford, turned out to be a typical Russian in spite of his English name. His father, he said, was English, but he had lived many years in Russia, first as an engineer in an English-owned munitions factory in Petrograd, and later in Riga. Jeff's mother was a Russian.

The strange adventures of this young man began when he was twenty-one years old, a date which corresponds with the outbreak of the world war. Jeff was counted as a Russian citizen and was forced to join the army. He saw service in the tragic campaign which ended in the Masurian Lakes catastrophe. He escaped drowning in the swamps and also lived through the disastrous retreat across East Prussia.

The Russians, he told me, fought well, their cavalry, one hundred thousand strong, breaking the German line and taking many prisoners. But the supporting artillery failed them; never came up at all. Mutiny broke out, many of the men charging that their higher officers had sold them out to the Germans. If this was so, then the Germans behaved toward their friends with their customary treachery. At one halt these Russian officers took possession of a German country house, obligingly left open and well furnished. Very soon after they were installed, the house blew up and killed every man in it. The place had been mined by the Germans.

In the Russian retreat, Jeff was taken prisoner, and with many others was sent first to Germany, where he was forced to slave at menial labor. Later he was sent to Belgium.

"I never let them know that I was a skilled mechanic," said he. "I didn't want to be set at munitions work, or to help them in any other way to win the war."

In Antwerp, Jeff, because he has a strong personality, was placed over a gang of Russians who were repairing streets. This was at a time when the British flyers were bombing Antwerp, and on one of their visits some of the bombs fell in a quarter of the town where this labor group was at work.

The German guards, to quote Jeff's exact words, "beat it to hell" for the nearest cellar, yelling to the prisoners to do the same. But Jeff and fifteen other Russians seized their chance and beat it to the water front. In the terror and excitement of the raid they were not stopped anywhere, and they managed to get hold of a fishing boat and beat it some more for the English Channel.

They had no food or water, but they thought they might be picked up, and after twelve anxious hours they were picked up by a Norwegian steamer. They were taken to London, and for a week or ten days were lionized and made much of. But of course they were Russian soldiers and had to be returned to their army. Jeff showed me the "paper" given him by the Russian consul in London, a safe conduct to the port where he was to embark for Norway and go from thence by rail to Russia.

Jeff kept the paper as a souvenir, but he had no intention of going home. Instead, with the aid of a Russian whom he had met in London, he went to quite another port and got a job as a stoker on a British merchant vessel bound for Marseilles, and from there to New York. By the time he reached New York he had eighty-five dollars in wages in his pocket.

He knew some English, and with true Russian facility, soon picked up more. He went to Coney Island one day, and there he scraped up an acquaintance with two soldiers of our regular army.

"Why not enlist?" they suggested, and Jeff, who was tired enough by this time to be tempted by an easy life and plenty to eat, consented. This was before we entered the war.

When the war came, however, Jeff was quite rested and perfectly game. He went to France with one of the first divisions, and is now in the artillery, which is showing the Huns something new and interesting, and is thereby earning the admiration of France and England.

As a matter of fact, when I met him he was acting as instructor in one of our big artillery camps. But he ached to get to the front, and by this time he must be there.

"Why were you willing to fight for America when you were not ready to go on fighting for Russia?" I asked him.

"In Russia the soldiers never get a square deal. In the American army they do," was the reply. "But that is not the only reason. There's something about America that makes you willing to do anything that is necessary. I guess it's because everybody feels free."

"But our army was drafted," I suggested. "Some people think that was an offense against individual freedom."

"Drafted, yes," said this real American, "but drafted to defend their individual freedom. Can't they see that?"

Jeff would be perfectly happy fighting for freedom if he only knew what fate had befallen his father and mother since the Russian upheaval. He has had no word from them since then, and he fears they have fallen victims to the bloody-handed Bolsheviki. His fine gray eyes filled with tears when he spoke of his mother, whom he left when he was little more than a boy. The chances are that he will never see her again.

We have thousands of Italian youths in our army. I talked with a handsome Italian sergeant, a well educated young man who had been a teller in an Italian bank in New York.

"You know what would make me the happiest man in the world?" he asked me. "It would be to be transferred to the Italian front with my whole company. I am a great admirer of the French and English, but of course I love Italy, and it would be great if we could go there, and in American uniforms, under the American flag, help to win back our Italia Irredenta, our Alsace-Lorraine.

"There are only four men in my company who were not born in Italy. Some of them were born in the lost provinces, and were naturalized as Austrians. But they hate Austria even more than they hate Germany. Think what it would mean to Italy to see her sons, who left her because they were poor, come back with the American army to fight for freedom on her soil."

I sincerely hope that these soldiers will be given a chance to fight in the land of their birth, under the flag that means freedom wherever it waves. Nothing would put more enthusiasm into the Italian army, in my opinion. Rightly or wrongly, the Italians, or some of them, have felt that the allies have neglected them a bit. Of course, German propaganda has worked overtime to make them feel that way, but there was, at one time, a slight basis for the feeling. I want to see American troops in Italy.

I want to see American troops on every front, and I particularly want to see the Czechs, the Bohemians, of whom we have great numbers in our army, fighting the Austrians. I saw some of these men, and they were magnificent soldiers.

I think the most uproariously happy men I saw in France were the Poles in our army. On the night I embarked at "a port in France" an American transport came in carrying, besides our khaki clad men, the Polish regiment recruited here last winter. They looked like the chorus of a musical comedy, but if they can fight as well as they can yell, they will add a chapter to the history of the war. They began to howl for joy when the ship came into the harbor, and they streamed down the gangplank singing and cheering like mad. I suppose their blue and scarlet uniforms have been put in moth balls by now.

We have often called America the melting pot, but, seeing this great multitude of foreign-born American soldiers, it occurred to me that we had not, in former years, kept a good enough fire burning under that pot. We didn't try hard enough to melt that mass, to amalgamate it with our Mayflower and Puritan descendants. Why is it that so many naturalized American citizens, fighting under the Stars and Stripes, speak no English, or very little? What have our public schools been doing all these years? Why haven't they extended their night school work to include these young men?

Russians, Austrians, Greeks, Italians, Chinese, Syrians, Turks, Africans (the American negro is just another immigrant), we have no right to keep America away from them. We do wrong to consider them only as "labor." They are American citizens, and for many of them the draft was the first time Uncle Sam ever called them son. The training camp was the real melting pot for them. In coin more precious than gold, those immigrant sons of America are paying us for our indifference. They are giving their lives for American ideals.

Read the names in the casualty lists: Killed in action, Private Alexandro Cassealeno, Private Mike Grba, Private Ole K. Arneson; severely wounded, Constantine Poniaros, Tony Kaczor, Alexander Mashewsky.

Many of these men were alone in America at the time of the draft. Their families were behind in the old home, and from some of those villages, those in the Austrian empire especially, no letters have come for more than a year. When the rest of the regiment gets letters and packages from home they get nothing. Remember that the next time they ask you to subscribe to the Red Cross, the Library War Service or the Salvation Army. You may think you haven't anybody in the war, no near relatives. But you are wrong, you have our foreign legion and you owe them everything you can possibly afford to give.

# CHAPTER X
# THE GENERAL HIMSELF

IF YOU talk with the American soldiers, as I did both in their rest billets and their camps, you will find they have the clearest and most definite understanding as to their business in Europe. It is to win the war. I never met a man who had the slightest doubt or hesitation about it. They know it will happen. They say to you: "Why, the general himself says so. 'Germany can and must be beaten.' The general himself said that."

"The general himself," of course, means General Pershing. He is to the American soldier what Foch is to the French *poilu*, the supreme authority who can not be mistaken. And to the French *poilu*, and to the French public at large, General Pershing, perhaps next to General Foch, is the commanding figure of the war. This in spite of the fact that they know nothing whatever of him as a fighting man. They believe in him, and in my opinion their faith is going to be justified.

"Character," said General Pershing, "other things being equal, will decide the last battle."

The basis of my confidence in General Pershing is that he has character, strong, original, dynamic. Every word and gesture reveals personality. He is absolutely straightforward and sincere, and his manner is simple and natural. Yet underneath that quiet simplicity you can easily perceive a will of steel and a capacity for great sternness. His first appearance won Paris completely, and before he has had time to fight a battle he has become a military hero in the eyes of the French.

I saw General Pershing first in the reception room of the beautiful Louis XVI mansion in the Rue de Varennes which has been loaned him for a town house when he goes to Paris. That is seldom. Most of the time he lives in a picturesque town in eastern France, which is the general headquarters of our army. The name of the town is almost never spoken. It is simply alluded to as G. H. Q. (General headquarters.)

Since the advent of the American forces in France there has been a much closer co-operation among the allies, a co-operation which reached its natural climax in the appointment of General Foch as generalissimo of the allied armies. France has long desired this arrangement, President Wilson desired it and so did Premier Lloyd George. General Pershing, in his swift, clear-minded judgment, declared it inevitable. But difficulties stood in the way of its accomplishment, and it was not until after several meetings of the allied war council at Versailles that the thing began to seem remotely possible.

In the interest of stronger co-operation and as commander-in-chief of the American army, General Pershing has been a constant attendant of the allied war councils. In a ten-minute interval between luncheon and departure for an afternoon session of the council, I had my first conversation with him. As he came into the room it occurred to me instantly that here was the very embodiment of the American army. The composite, the perfect type. No wonder the French like him. He *looks* right.

No Greek of old Sparta was ever a more perfect physical specimen. At fifty-four, General Pershing is as straight and slender of waist as when he left West Point. He is tall, powerful of frame, without an ounce of fat anywhere on his body, and as hard as bronze. His eyes are keen and young, although his hair is gray. His face is marked with a few deep, scar-like lines, for tragedy has entered his life, as all the world knows. The lines do not suggest age, however. General Pershing looks younger than his years, much younger than most of his published photographs. His voice is that of a young man, and he speaks crisply, without ever hesitating for a word.

There is not a particle of pose about Pershing. He has been called cold, but I did not find him so. When I told him that I had a son in the army he became decidedly cordial. What was the boy's name? His regiment? When did he reach France? Had I seen him? The commander-in-chief of the American army, on his way to an allied council with men who have the fate of civilization in their hands, had time to ask questions about an enlisted man. Lincoln used to do things like that.

Weeks later I was the guest, with several other correspondents, of the intelligence department of the army in a motor journey into our war zone. Our passes were for three days only and three districts were to be visited. One stopping place was the town alluded to as G. H. Q., the heart of the American expeditionary force in France. We were to meet the commander-in-chief informally, but there was to be no interview. The prospect was pleasing, but not particularly exciting, and in that it matched up pretty well with the rest of the trip. When the intelligence department invites correspondents, especially women correspondents, to a party you can be sure that it is a very staid and conservative affair.

We traveled by train from Paris to our first point, a big camp where our engineers had done some wonders of construction, and which was now a completely equipped school, where thousands of soldiers were being trained in bombing, trench mortar work and other skilled branches. At the station we were met by a handsome and diplomatic young intelligence officer in a big limousine. Under his chaperonage we were to see as much of the war zone as was considered good for us. The second day brought us to G. H. Q. and General Pershing.

Then was I glad that I had seen him in the palace in the Rue de Varennes. Because now I knew something about him. I knew he liked candor and straight talk. I knew also that with an inflexible will he possessed a reasonable mind. You can argue with a man like that. I did argue with General Pershing on the subject of what women correspondents ought to be permitted to see and to know. I told him what I wanted to take back to the mothers of American soldiers.

I can not repeat our conversation, because it was confidential. I will simply say that General Pershing proved the reasonableness of his mind by greatly extending our facilities on that trip, and turning our prim little party into an experience wholly worth while from the reporter's point of view. Later I shall go into details about that trip up the line. This chapter is concerned with General Pershing.

In the plain bare room, which is the commander's private headquarters, and in which the great campaigns which our men will fight are being planned, General Pershing appears even more dynamic and forceful than in his luxurious Parisian home. I have seen generals who wore their uniforms as if they were business clothes, but not so General Pershing. If he wore business clothes he would contrive to make them look like a uniform. His uniform is the most immaculate, the most correct, the most military thing in the way of garments that I have ever beheld. His boots look as though he never wore the same pair a second time. Yet there is nothing stiff or rigid in his appearance. He puts his clothes on a perfect masculine figure, that is all. He holds himself like an absolutely fit and athletic man.

General Pershing exalts health. He takes daily cold baths, one of his young aides told me, and often in the dead of winter runs and exercises in the open air clad only in a thin bathrobe. To bring every man in the army up to his physical standard is the commander's expressed ambition. To make them supremely healthy, efficient fighting men, and to return them to their mothers morally as well as physically sound, is General Pershing's conception of his responsibility as head of the American army.

It is always interesting to know how we appear in the eyes of strangers, and an article published in a well-known French magazine shows the strong appeal that General Pershing has made to the imagination of our allies. According to the French writer, there are two men in the American commander-in-chief, one of them Anglo-Saxon, the other a Frenchman. In 1749 the ancestors of General Pershing emigrated from Alsace to America, and Alsace in the eyes of all Frenchmen is and always will be France.

If by rare favor you are received by General Pershing in his Paris home you meet the Anglo-Saxon, says the reporter. There his coldness is positively British. "Tall, slender as a sublieutenant, well set up in his khaki brown uniform, four stars on the shoulders and on the collar the golden eagle of his supreme rank. General Pershing receives you in a manner courteous but glacial. He is entirely the official, conscious of his great responsibilities, and determined to keep silence concerning official matters. His blue eyes are clear and cold, even hard. Above his strong jaw, indicative of implacable energy, his lips, saber-straight, wear no smile.

"Do not attempt to get from him any details of his mission in France, or try to induce him to give you any personal souvenirs or anecdotes of his tour of the French front. His aide-de-camp and interpreter has an invariable reply to all such questions: 'The general has nothing to say.' Above all, never venture to ask a question concerning his private life, his joys or sorrows. Immediately the look in his cold eyes becomes hostile. Before the question is fairly out the answer comes: 'The general does not think that would interest the public.'

"But if by happy circumstance you are privileged to enter the small circle of General Pershing's friends, what a delightful metamorphosis! The man reveals himself simple, charming, pliant, spontaneous. He is the Frenchman, cordial and communicative, ready to lend himself to that juvenile gaiety which so much amuses the Anglo-Saxon. The blue eyes that we have seen flash so coldly are now at once mischievous and tender. His features are animated, his smile ready.

"Everything interests him, science, art, literature. Music he loves almost as well as paintings, and he tells you with what new pleasure every time he visited the Paris of pre-war days he went each day to the Louvre galleries. Above all, he tells you how profoundly happy he is to be in the war on our side. Certainly that joy is rooted in the satisfaction of a soldier fulfilling his duty, but General Pershing is more than a soldier. He is an idealist called to accomplish a high mission, to serve an unselfish cause, to help humanity to a secure and happy future."

General Pershing never appeared a bigger man than when he offered to brigade the American forces in with the English and the French, and himself take the subordinate position of a commander without a real command. The offer was made and accepted in the dark and panic-ridden early days of the March German offensive, when it looked as though the allied lines might be broken, and all the man power available had to be mobilized.

That danger is happily past. The Germans have struck and the blow has proved utterly futile. The Americans are to be allowed to fight under their own flag and their own officers. They will get full credit for what they do. But the French and English will never forget that General Pershing was unselfishly willing, when necessary, to forego both for himself and the American army every particle of credit, letting the honors go to the allies. From a man of that character great fighting, splendid victories may be expected. Under such a commander our sons are well secured.

---

# CHAPTER XI
# GENERAL ALLAIRE'S FINEST

"I KNOW that my boy is being well cared for in his regiment, and I'm not afraid of what may happen to him as long as he is on duty. But what about his off hours? What is to prevent him from falling into bad company?"

I know that this thought has troubled the minds of many mothers of soldiers now in France. And no wonder. Ever since the first training camps were set up in this country the most lurid tales have been spread abroad about the alleged immorality of the soldiers' off hours. Some of these tales were spread by pro-Germans, pacifists and cowards who hoped to defeat the draft laws. Others were the result of a certain kind of imagination. The vast majority of them were untrue.

But even if any of them were true, if boys of twenty-one, away from the restraining influences of home, found unusual opportunities for immorality right here in the United States, what must it be in France? Many American women have it firmly fixed in their minds that France is a shocking immoral country. It isn't, but I do not hope to be able to unsettle the conviction.

I will content myself with saying that even if France were a second Sodom or Gomorrah, our soldiers would be safe there. As safe, or safer, than they would be at home. The reason is that they are under military discipline and military supervision every hour of their lives. In their off hours they are supervised by the most efficient and powerful police force in the world, the military police of the American army.

Military police is what we call them for short. They are really assistant provost marshals. They are everywhere in France where there are American soldiers. They police Paris and all other cities, towns and villages in our zone. They are found sitting at a little table in all the railroad stations, and every traveling American soldier, be he officer, non-com or private, has to report the minute he arrives to the station marshal. This applies to all holders of military passes, Red Cross and Y. M. C. A. workers, and war correspondents.

The marshal examines the papers of the traveling officer or soldier, stamps them and enters the name and destination of the traveler in his book. This happens when the soldier leaves his base and when he returns. They keep track of our men on all their travels.

They also keep track of our soldiers in their daily walks abroad, whether on duty or pleasure bent. There are certain rules in our expeditionary force which apply to all alike, from General Pershing down to Bill Smith, private, just arrived from Camp Funston or Camp Upton. One of these rules is that no member of the expeditionary force may associate with women of the submerged class.

If a military policeman sees an officer or a soldier in such company it is his duty immediately and without any delay to separate the two, and gather the offending man in. If he fails to do so, and the fact is established, the policeman is punished. But he doesn't fail.

Some of our younger officers, only a few, I was assured, didn't believe at first that a simple private soldier would dare arrest them for the offense of having a "good time." Two of these very new lieutenants tested it out in Paris once. They annexed a pair of women of the underworld and started out to find whatever may be left of the night life of the French capital.

What was their indignation when a slim youth of about twenty-three, wearing the uniform of a private, with the sole addition of a brassard marked A. P. M., walked up to them, saluted and stepped politely between them and the open door of the taxi-cab.

"Beg pardon, sirs," he said courteously, "I am obliged to remind you that you are transgressing the provisions of section —— of regulation —— of orders —— relating to associations with women. I shall have to request you to accompany me to headquarters."

The two very new young officers declined the invitation, first with indignation, then with good-natured appeals to the soldier's sporting blood. The soldier remained adamant, and then one of the officers, getting genuinely angry, thrust his fist under the man's nose. "What would you do if I were to push your face in and go on my way?"

The soldier policeman promptly drew his automatic and thrust it under the lieutenant's nose. "I would do my duty, sir," he replied, still courteously. But he was an American and couldn't hold in any longer. "By God," he exclaimed, "I wish you'd try it on. You're the kind of an officer the American army could afford to lose suddenly."

That settled it. The two officers went to headquarters, and they were punished. The one that attempted to frighten the young policeman got sent back to the United States. The men at headquarters agreed with the policeman that the United States army could afford to lose a man like that.

The military policeman, who is found all over our zone in France, does not wear blue clothes and a peaked cap. Neither does he carry a baton. He wears his soldier uniform and a white arm band on which the letters A. P. M., assistant provost marshal, appear in letters of red. He wears a belt and a pistol and he carries plenty of ammunition with him.

He is a part of a service which has at its head General Allaire, chief provost marshal of the army, one of General Pershing's staff. General Allaire lives at the sequestered little town which houses the rest of the staff. Under him are many officers who command the regiments of assistant provost marshals, and they are held responsible for the order and good conduct of the army.

In Paris the military police have their headquarters in an old-fashioned building in the Rue Ste. Anne, close to the heart of old Paris. The place was a hotel in pre-war days, and it looks very much like a hotel now, with all the boarders in uniform. The big dining-room has less style about it than formerly. At present it is furnished with long pine tables, scrubbed clean, and the dishes are mostly white enamel ware.

A one-armed French soldier, with a most engaging smile and a pretty good knowledge of English, acts as elevator boy, and he told me once that when the war was over he was going to America. "I want to know how it feels," he said, "to belong, even for part of my life, to a country that can produce such boys as these."

They are a picked lot. It is an honor to be in the service, and only those in whose honor as well as valor the authorities have the greatest confidence, ever make the service.

In Paris the lieutenant under whose direct command the force works is the most single-minded man I think I have ever met. His whole existence seems bound up in his men. He even spends his off hours with them. One Monday when I went to the house in the Rue Ste. Anne to have a military pass stamped by the proper provost marshal, this lieutenant of police told me that the day before, Sunday, he had taken the half of his men who were off duty to Versailles. They had a wonderful day, he said. The authorities even opened the palace museum for the Americans.

"Next Sunday," he said, "I am going to take the other half of the force down the Seine to a beautiful place where we can have dinner out-of-doors and have a look at French life of the old régime. I mean that my men shall get all there is in a foreign sojourn."

I told him that I thought he was pretty fine to give all his leisure to his soldiers. He blushed like a boy and said: "They deserve it and I enjoy it. Besides, it is a part of my job to make these men as intelligent individuals as possible. They need to be intelligent. They have eight hours a day of particularly responsible work.

"Here in Paris they have to keep their eyes out for deserters. It is their business to know that every American soldier who walks through a street here has a right to do it. They have to be keen to look for spies in American uniforms. Oh, yes, they have picked up more than a few of these gentry. They might have slipped past the French soldiers, because they don't know Americans, but they couldn't fool a U. S. A. P. M. Every suspicious character gets nabbed sooner or later. If there is any doubt about his status our men bring him in here. If he can satisfy us, all right. But there is never an apology due him from the policeman.

"One of our men may be transferred from patrol work to riding on railroad trains and keeping track of our soldiers on their travels. He may be transferred to the front, where he becomes a traffic cop and also one of the men who take captured Germans in charge.

"We have a school here for our motorcycle cops. These men become inspectors of police. They have an added responsibility. They speed directly to the scene of any great or small disaster, and they assist the French gendarmes and military police. When the long-distance gun hit that church on Good Friday, killing seventy-six people, our men were the first on the spot. They rescued the wounded and brought out the dead. They also did excellent service in that great fire near Paris when the powder works blew up.

"As quickly as an air raid is over our men are out on their cycles looking up the damage inflicted by the bombs. They report back here where every bomb fell. Often they are able to put out small fires caused by the bombs.

"They are a fine bunch," ended the lieutenant. "Not one of my men has ever been in trouble, and the fact that our cooler here in Paris often has as many as a hundred and fifty people in it shows not only that their work is essential, but that it is performed to the king's taste."

With that kind of a police force and that kind of officers commanding it, you can be sure that your sons haven't very much opportunity to go astray. Once in a while a man may evade the military police. Occasionally I have seen it done. But it happens rarely, and the chances are a hundred to one against it happening twice to any one man.

# CHAPTER XII
# INTO THE TRENCHES

THERE comes a day when our sons cease to be soldiers in training and become fighting men. It is a day looked forward to with dread by those at home, with eager enthusiasm by the soldiers. I have seldom met a soldier who had not something uncomplimentary to say of the powers for not sending him more promptly to the front. The weeks spent in rest billets, that is, the training camps, seem endless to the men. Every move forward is hailed with joy. But progress from one village to the next is exasperatingly slow, especially after they reach a point where the rumble of guns, like distant thunder, is heard.

I can answer for it that those distant guns do not terrify anybody. I have listened to them, and I had the same impulse to push on, on, nearer, which besets the men. There is a real intoxication in the sound. It intrigues you, fills you with a kind of savage curiosity, a desire to send back to that challenge a Gargantuan defiance. At this stage of the soldier's career I know that he thoroughly enjoys himself. I have been that far with the American army myself and I can testify that everybody had a good time.

Shortly after our men took over their first sector on what is known as the Toul front, I was privileged to travel for several days directly behind this front in an army motor-car. The Toul sector was a part of the French front in a northeastern corner of the country drained by two historic rivers, the Meuse and the Moselle. Toul itself is an ancient walled town with a magnificent cathedral and a moat still in working order. Some sixty kilometers, or less than thirty-eight miles to the northeast, lies immortal Verdun, and eastward almost in a straight line is Nancy, the lovely capital of old Lorraine. Nancy is so close to the German lines that it has been bombed and raided many times. When I saw it the people were spending much of their time in bomb-proof cellars constructed for their protection by the municipality.

How tenaciously the French cling to their homes was evident long before I reached Nancy. Spring was in the air in spite of cold wind and a wet clinging snow that fell and dripped through three or four disagreeable days. The fields surrounding the low villages had been freshly plowed, and here and there we saw gnarled peasants, old men and women, who stolidly dug and harrowed, just as their grandparents did when Frederick "the Great" raided the border near these very farms. Just as their ancestors did during ceaseless wars of old.

Straight and white for miles ran the ribboned highroads between their avenues of tall poplars. But as we progressed farther north, the roads began to be cut up with great holes worn by heavy war trucks and gun carriages. Fields to the right and left put on a strange and sinister dress. Here were no peasants plowing, for those fields blossomed with a harvest of barbed wire entanglements, mazes of barbed wire so wound and woven, so thick and strong that only repeated shellings by heavy artillery could level them. To me they looked like some devilish parody of the rich vineyards I had seen only recently terracing the hills of southern France.

A little farther on the fields were lined and crossed not only with barbed wire but with trenches, neatly dug and lined with a basketwork of willow withes. These trenches so far behind the lines amazed me. "Surely the Germans could not get as far as this," I protested.

"Probably not," said the officer who was our escort, "but we are not taking any chances. Suppose our men were forced to retreat fighting. Well, here are rear defenses all ready for them."

My son being at that moment in Toul, waiting to go forward, I conceived a positive affection for those trenches, and the barbed wire entanglements began suddenly to look benevolent.

Our motor-car was no longer alone on the long highroad leading northward. We traveled now in company with many olive drab motor-trucks and ambulances, all with U. S. A. and a string of identity numbers painted in white letters on the sides. We passed many mule teams, the melancholy mules wearing around their necks the grotesque gas mask which is a part of their harness over there. Groups of foot soldiers, some French but mostly American, hailed us as we passed. Others we saw alongside of the road digging and draining. The road, built high above the surrounding fields, was hard and dry, but the country was a bog of mud and water.

Our objective was a village, too small to deserve a name on any but a war map. It is important because it was the distributing point along this particular sector, for American troops and army supplies. It is about the last village up the line where one may safely venture without a gas mask. The road leading to the village, and the main street when we turned into it, were choked with motor-trucks, cars, ambulances, mules and men, thousands of men, in brown uniforms and steel helmets.

As we wormed our way through this maze of heavy traffic, and as I stepped out of the car into mud a foot deep, I had a remarkable mental experience. My imagination suddenly switched back to a warm November day in New York. I stood on a corner of Fifth Avenue and watched, with half a million others, a regiment of drafted men starting for training camp on Long Island. New York was giving the men a great farewell, bands, flags, cheers, and from the marble balcony of the Union Club a reviewing party of distinguished men, some of them veterans of the Civil War.

The marching men were a pretty weedy and ill-conditioned lot, city bred, most of them, indoor workers looking less than their average of twenty-three years. They struggled and panted under their burden of suit-cases, canvas kit bags, bundles and other receptacles. Their faces wore expressions of anxiety and fatigue, and a few looked actually terror stricken. In the crowds that lined the avenue were many women, mothers, wives and sweethearts of the men, and their suffering was often pitiful to see and to hear. Above the blare of the bands their voices floated shrilly:

"There he is—there's Henry. Oh, my God!"

"Abie! Ach mein sohn!"

"Oh! Oh! Isn't it too horrible? All those boys going to their death!"

What brought me that sudden acute vision of memory was the complete contrast of the facts and what those suffering women had foreseen as facts. Also the astonishing contrast between the drafted recruit and the soldier a few months' work had created. Nowhere in the United States had I ever seen anything like the husky young lieutenants who were being introduced to me, and a few minutes later were escorting me through the mud to the cottage where I was to have lunch. We ate in a stone-flagged kitchen furnished with a table, some rough wooden chairs and an old oak dresser that would have tempted a collector. There was a huge fireplace, in the chimney of which hung a dozen hams and bacons, and some garlickly sausages, all smoking in the fire of poplar logs. The walls were hung with highly colored pictures of saints and martyrs.

The food was good and there were mountains of it. Beef stew, fried potatoes, beans, vegetables, bread and butter, a pudding with raisins and a wine sauce, cups and cups of hot coffee. Every one from the captain down ate prodigiously, for it was the last sit-down-at-a-table meal the men were going to enjoy for at least two weeks. Their corps was starting for the trenches within an hour.

After lunch I hurried out to take a look at the relieving party of soldiers, standing at ease on one side of the narrow street. They were drafted men, not regulars, and this was to be their first taste of fighting, their baptism of fire, as men have termed it. The far sound of guns that troubled the air was all they knew of artillery. Two weeks from that hour they would know more. They would be able to distinguish between one gun and another, and to name each one as it roared. They would have all the slang names, the

Minnie Wurfer, the Dolly Sisters, that explode more than once as they fly, the typewriters, as they call machine guns. Now they knew only a distant growl, menacing, warning, inviting. Were they ready, our men?

Physically they were ready. You could see that. Men who six or eight months ago would have sent for an express wagon to carry more than a suit-case, stood up there in the icy mud straight and clean and hard as nails. Their chests filled their coats to the bulging point, and on their backs they carried without strain or effort between sixty and seventy pounds of equipment. Each man carried, besides his gun and ammunition, half a tent, a haversack of clothing, a mess kit, a trench tool, a gas mask, a bayonet, a knapsack of food, a water bottle, an extra pair of heavy, hob-nailed boots, and a few other miscellaneous articles of his own choosing.

"The blankets and really heavy things go on the trucks," explained one of the lieutenants. "The men carry with them no more than they would absolutely have to have in case they were taken prisoner, extra clothing and personal effects, I mean. A man who falls into the hands of the Germans needs extra shirts, socks and boots. You bet, Fritz hasn't any to spare."

Then I saw that the men of our army were ready indeed. At this frank suggestion of possible capture by a cruel foe did they shudder and turn pale? They did not. They grinned and wagged their absurd tin hats and said: "You betcha," and "You said it." They were as unconcerned as though they were waiting for a subway train instead of army trucks headed for the trenches. Months of training, outdoor living, regular habits, obedience to orders, devotion to an idea, have worked this physical and spiritual miracle with our draft army. The men are as strong as the Rooseveltian bull moose. They are hardened to mud and cold and wildest weather, and their nerves are as steady as an old clock.

Nearly four years ago the splendid armies of Belgium and France rushed into the fray, the magnificent volunteer army of Great Britain joining them in swift order. But none of those armies were quite like ours. Those men went out, without adequate training, in a passion of patriotism, in a glory of rage and pain. Their hearts were blazing, their brains on fire. They knew that they must die if their countries were to live. The American soldiers are fired by no such strong emotion. The men I saw in France, on their way to the trenches, were like men going to work. There was a fight ahead of them, and a possibility of wounds and death. Well, that was their job, like mining, or bridge building, or turning virgin soil to make a home. They faced it calmly and conscientiously, and while they waited they made casual conversation with the last woman they would see for weeks, the last woman some of them would ever see.

"I seen you down at Aix-lay-Beans a while back, didn't I?" remarked a tall Texan, holding out a big hand for me to clasp. "Ain't that some town? Before that I used to think this here France was nothing but a mud-hole. What do they want to fight for such a country, I used to say. Let the Dutchies have it, I said, and let they-all move to Texas."

"Yeah," agreed a black-eyed, husky young Hebrew from the east side of New York. "I used to think like that. It cost a lot of money to go to Aix, but it was worth it every cent. Who wouldn't fight to keep those mountains and those grape fields running up them like a regular park?"

A young man with a Georgia address stenciled on his knapsack asked me where I came from, and when I told him he said that I certainly looked like a southerner. Anyhow I favored a young lady in Atlanta to whom he was very partial. He hadn't seen Aix-les-Bains, but give him Atlanta for a sure enough city. He was going to live there after the war.

All of them expected to live through the war. Not one of them was murmuring prayers, not one charged me with any farewell messages. A young chap who said that he belonged to the 1919 class of Chicago University urged me quite earnestly not to leave the village without sampling the doughnuts fried fresh every day by the girls in the Salvation Army hut directly back of us. "They fry nearly fifteen hundred every day," he told me, "and not a doughnut lasts long enough to get cold."

"How do you feel about going out to kill your first Germans?" I asked curiously.

They were not going to let me know how delighted they were to get into "the show" at last. They put on a magnificent air of indifference. "Got to begin sometime," said one, "might as well begin now." "If we don't hustle some the French and English will finish the war without us," said another. "Then how'd we feel?" The eagerest reply I got was from a strong-armed youth from Wyoming. "That's what we're here for, ain't we?" he exclaimed. "We're here to kill Germans, and I say, for the love of Mike, cut out some of the drill and let us fight." I wish I could reproduce the way he spoke that last word, fight.

"Don't you kind of dread the cold and wet of the trenches?" I asked, banteringly. The men laughed, they roared. "Say, lady," called one man, "the trenches haven't got a darn thing on the barns we've been sleeping in since last October." They laughed again and the mirth spread to the juvenile population of the village which, practically intact, hung fondly around chewing American gum. "Good night," shrilled the children. It is the only English expression the French juvenile has acquired, and he uses it on all occasions.

It was Sunday afternoon and across the narrow street the bells of the village church began to ring for vespers. The curé, a tall, fine French priest, came striding down the street, the skirts of his soutaine held high out of the mud. With his free hand he swept off his hat to the soldiers, calling *au revoirs* as he passed. At the same time he rounded up as many of the gum-chewing youngsters as he could, shooing them ahead of him into the darkness of the old church.

The bell ceased its impatient clamor, and as if the bell had been a tocsin, the village street became the scene of sudden, intense activity. Orders were roared out and were repeated down the long line. The men sprang to attention, moving like some dynamic piece of machinery. Trucks began to wind and move noisily toward the highway. Whips cracked, mules brayed, sirens sounded, and before I fairly realized what had happened the men were on the march.

Snow was falling, first lightly, then in a dense cloud. I watched the soldiers disappear quickly as in a thick mist. Soon even the chug of their feet tramping through the mud was lost. The village street was empty save of mire and falling snow. And in my heart was so much bursting pride that there was no more room for any meaner emotions of pity or of fear.

# CHAPTER XIII
## WRITE TO HIM OFTEN—BUT

ONE morning, in a big American camp in France, I witnessed the arrival of a long-delayed batch of mail from home. No words of mine can describe how joyfully it was received. Officers and men alike were children in their happiness. They sang and shouted while the letters and parcels were being distributed, and afterward a deep silence fell on the camp while the letters were being read.

Alas for those who received no letters that day. My heart ached for them, and I want to urge, as part of the patriotic duty of every citizen, that as far as possible no soldier is neglected in this respect. Every man and woman with a relative or friend in the army, and this will soon mean practically every citizen of the United States, ought to write frequently to their soldiers.

If you haven't time to write long letters, write short ones. If you haven't time for short letters, write postcards. But write something.

As soon as the men go to training camp begin to write to them. Nearly every soldier has a period of bewilderment and homesickness, and this usually occurs early in his military career. Young, so young, most of our splendid soldiers, many of whom when they are drafted leave home for the first time in their lives. It does not do to risk breaking the home ties altogether.

One of the things that burden the hearts of our English allies is the fear that this may have happened in the case of a great many of the brave Australian and New Zealand soldiers. They are incredibly remote from their homes. It takes letters three months to cross the immense waste of waters that lie between those south Pacific islands and the French battle-fields. Three months for a mother to answer a question asked her by her son. Six months for an exchange of words between a husband and wife.

Thousands of the Anzacs have been away from home, been separated from their families for three years. When they have leave of absence they go to England, and clubs and canteens have been opened for them in London and elsewhere. But their home ties are never knit. The English fear that in many, many cases they will never knit again.

We do not want that to happen to our soldiers and the best, indeed the only way to prevent it, is to write letters, frequent letters, and the right kind of letters.

I watched those soldiers in our camp overseas reading their letters from home. They did not read them just once and then fold them up and put them in their pockets. Every letter was read a dozen times over, until the words were learned by heart. That is why it is so important that the right kind of letters be written.

Don't write, "The interest on the mortgage is due again next week and I'm sure I don't know where the money is coming from." Don't tell your boys that you have had a bad spell of neuralgia and can hardly see to write. Don't tell him that Jennie is doing badly in school and shows a sulky temper. Those are your worries, not his. He has responsibilities ahead of him, and possibly troubles and suffering immeasurably bigger than anything you face.

Above all, never deplore the fact that he is in the war, and never tell him that you are praying for an early peace. No American soldier whose mind has been enlightened to the true state of affairs in this war wants an early peace. He knows that an early peace would be a dangerous, a fatal, peace, one pleasing only to the Germans and their starving and enslaved allies.

In all the neutral countries, but even more in the allied countries, German propaganda is working overtime to bring about an early peace. German agents are everywhere trying to undermine the morale of the allied people, especially the women, and through them the soldiers. How they get into France is a mystery, but they get there, and they often remain undetected for a long time.

I remember visiting in the home of a simple bourgeois French family where the one remaining soldier son was home on leave. Three sons of that family had given up their lives for France, one at the Marne, one at Verdun, and one in the first battle of the Somme. The one remaining son was in a dangerous service, and perhaps one can hardly blame his mother and sisters for listening to any suggestion of a possible peace.

They had heard, one of the sisters said, as we sat at tea, without cream or cakes, or even bread, that France and Austria were about to sign a separate peace. They hoped the news was true, because then Italy would make peace, and the allies would only have to fight the Germans in France and Flanders.

"Never, my dear sister," said the resolute young French soldier, "listen to any talk of that kind. Never repeat it, especially in the hearing of a soldier. We have our work to do, and you must help us, not weaken us. There is only one kind of peace we want, and that is the peace that will come when Germany is conquered."

He got up from his seat and left the room, returning soon with a poster, one of the many beautiful and striking war posters the French have produced. This one showed a terrible procession of old men, women and children being driven from their homes by the advance of German troops. The Germans were striking the helpless people with the flat of their swords and laughing brutally at their sufferings.

"This is no fiction," said the French soldier to me. "This is fact. And this is what would happen again in a few years if we made peace too soon. Why not end it for all time now? We men are ready to give our lives. We embrace the earth when we fall, for the sacrifice of a few lives now is nothing to the horrors that are in store for our children to come, unless we win, really win, this war."

I said: "I will tell the American people what you have said, and what I know to be true, for I have seen something of this war, and I know what might happen in my country unless we win a complete victory."

Because I am particularly concerned lest our women unwittingly weaken the least bit the morale and the fighting spirit of our soldiers, I am going to tell them what I have seen.

My only son, I have said before, is a soldier. He is at the front. Yet, after what I have seen of this war, I would never speak of peace to him. I don't want him to think of peace. I want him to think of fighting.

Since this war began, nearly two million people, not fighters, but women and children and men too old and infirm to fight, have been driven in wretchedness from their homes. This in France alone.

We know what happened in Belgium, in Serbia, in Roumania and Poland. Armenia? Words fail in describing what happened there. I have seen only France, and I can speak only of France. Two million French people have fled before fire and sword.

But that isn't anything very terrible, by comparison. To lose your home and everything you possess is a bearable thing—by comparison. On a Sunday soon after the great spring battle began I spent the day in a railroad station at a junction where hundreds of trains rushed ceaselessly to the north bearing soldiers and munitions, and to the south with wounded men, refugees and broken guns and airplanes. Many refugees were fed and comforted by the French Red Cross at the station that day.

It was my privilege to help a little those noble French women. I filled hundreds of cups with coffee, strong and hot, and I helped to feed the exhausted who could not even stand up at the counter where coffee and sandwiches were served. We literally fed them, holding the food to their lips.

There was one old woman—perhaps she was not really old, but her sufferings had emaciated her and seamed her face with wrinkles—who was my special care for an hour. She had to be given brandy before she could sit up, and she had to be fed hot milk from a spoon, like a baby. She was almost dead. Another woman, her neighbor in the ruined and violated village that once was their home, told me in quick whispers that old woman's story.

When the Germans invaded France in August, 1914, this woman lived in a small town directly in the path of the Wurtemburg army that swept in from Lorraine. Her husband kept a small shop where tobacco and fruit and such like were sold. They had a home and three children—Cécile, sixteen; Georges, twelve, and Marcel, six. They were quiet people, like all the other villagers, and the mobilizing of their men when war came was the first great and terrifying event in their lives. This woman's husband had a club foot and could not be mobilized. She had no son old enough to fight, so she was counted lucky.

Then the Germans came. They swarmed in early one morning and the horrified villagers at once began to see war in its most frightful guise. Soldiers broke into the home of the club-footed man and demanded tobacco. He led the way to his little shop and told them to help themselves. They did, and when they had filled their pockets and their haversacks they shot the lame man through the heart. Meantime, with torch and grenade, other soldiers were setting fire to the village. They burned the dead tobacconist's home, and when the wife rushed from the house with her youngest child in her arms they shot the child. He screamed "Mother!" just once, and died.

She and her two remaining children fled, but Cécile, the sixteen-year-old daughter, did not get very far. She was seized by a German officer, and it was a year before her mother saw her again. When those two met again the girl was a skeleton, and she bore in her arms a skeleton baby. It was a girl. Otherwise they would not have permitted her to take it back to France.

The reunited family made their way to a relative in a village near Peronne. When the Germans swept over that district in 1916 they fled again, and in the flight Cécile, never strong after her experience in Germany, died. Soon afterward the baby died. Georges, now a sturdy boy of fourteen, was all that was left. After the Germans retreated last November they went back to their village near Peronne, and the boy worked for their support—until March twenty-first, this year. Then they fled again, and here she was— alone.

"Where is Georges?" I asked.

"Do not speak so loud, madame," implored the neighbor. "The poor one can not be told just yet, but Georges was killed by a shell that burst near the station when we got on the train. Not all of us could get on that train. She thinks that Georges was left behind and that he will come to-morrow."

I could write stories like that to fill a book. Indeed, it has been done, officially done, by the French government, and every story was carefully authenticated before it was published. I tell this story because it was told to me while I was feeding the wretched victim.

I speak only of what I know, and I know that this woman, one of thousands, is just a type, an example, of what has happened, what is happening to-day, but what must never happen again. The only way to prevent it happening again, perhaps to our American women, is to put out of the world the thing Germany stands for and which she is fighting desperately to keep alive and powerful.

---

# CHAPTER XIV
# WHEN THEY WIN WOUND STRIPES

SOMEWHERE in France the soldier son for whom I wear my service pin lies wounded. A few hours before I sat down to write these words I heard the news, and almost as soon as the first shock had passed I thought to myself how much worse I should feel did I not know what wonderful things were being done for him at that hour. I said, I must hurry, hurry, and tell all the women I can reach, other women whose sons have been wounded, some of the reasons why I can think about my soldier with a heart full of quiet confidence.

My Julian was one of the splendid regiments of young untried American soldiers who on May twenty-eighth stormed their way into the village of Cantigny, and who, in spite of repeated German counter-attacks, have held that part of the line like a stone wall ever since.

It was only a minor engagement, to be sure, but it was so gallantly fought that it gained the highest admiration of the French and British commanders. It showed the civilized world what was going to happen when the American army got over in full force. I am proud to have had a son in that glorious fight at Cantigny.

He went over the top with his comrades into the face of a murderous machine-gun fire. He must have been in the front ranks, for he was among the first to fall. "I tried to keep on going," he told the New York *World* correspondent who saw him in the hospital, "but it was no use. I had to flop."

Two hours he lay helpless in No Man's Land, shells bursting near him, and with the prospect of being bayoneted if the Germans were allowed to regain that ground. I don't let myself think about those two hours. I know, all too well, what they must have been like. I won't think about the pain of the wounded leg, nor the burning sun, the tormenting thirst, the anxiety and impatience before the stretcher bearers came. The wounded, thank God, soon forget all these, and so must we at home.

I had not heard directly from my son since the beginning of this great second battle of the Somme. I was very near his division for a time, and was never much farther away than Paris until I sailed for home, but no letters came through. I was like hundreds of thousands of other women here in America in not knowing whether my soldier was in action or out of danger in the rear.

Now that I know I am glad, for I sympathized with his intense desire to have a first-hand share in this war of liberation. When we entered the war my son was too young for the draft, and in fact he would only this spring have been called upon to register. Knowing that he might have to wait a year and a half before going over, he enlisted in the old army and went to France in one of the earliest units. He had to take service in a working contingent, and like all those valuable but usually non-combatant soldiers he feared that he would never be given a chance to fight. I am very grateful that they gave him his chance, and so soon. I have seen something of the work of the unspeakable Hun. Since then I have never been sorry for our fighting men. The only men I am sorry for are those who live in these times and never have a chance to join the allied armies.

I am thankful that my son lived through his first battle, and I am especially relieved to hear that he went to an American hospital. I have visited many of those hospitals in France, and I am going to devote this chapter to telling other women who have wounded men over there how our soldiers are cared for when German gun-fire strikes them down. I can not think of anything else to-day, nor write of anything else.

The wounded are picked up as quickly as possible, the stretcher bearers and ambulance men working bravely under fire, and often in great danger. All musicians, military bandsmen, are stretcher bearers, and the same service is part of the work of the medical corps. They bring the wounded to what are called advance dressing stations or regimental aid posts, directly behind the lines. These stations indeed are in the trenches, and the doctors work to the noise of bursting shells and exploding shrapnel. In these trench dressing stations minor wounds are dressed, and first aid is given to the seriously injured.

One very important thing is done in the first aid posts. Every wounded man is inoculated against tetanus. Lockjaw—that most horrible of all wound complications—is now practically a thing of the past. Our hospitals will possibly never see a case, because our surgeons take immediate precautions against it.

In these advanced aid posts they also take precautions against wound shock, the mysterious cause of many deaths in this war. One of the first symptoms of wound shock is cold and the surgeons and dressers have hot, sweet tea on hand and many blankets. Patients are given cups of hot tea as soon as they come in, and if the weather is cold they are wrapped up like Eskimos before they are sent on.

About wounded men in general, I want to say that the great majority are only slightly injured. They are all conscientiously treated, even small scratches being dressed carefully, because every wound is an infected wound and if neglected might cause death. But most of the casualties are able to walk back to their next base, the field or evacuation hospital. Those who are seriously wounded are transported in ambulances.

The field hospital is located near the battle line, but out of range of the guns. They are near enough, however, to be vulnerable to the gentlemanly boches, who make a specialty of dropping aerial bombs on wounded soldiers and women nurses. We have had tendered us by the French government a number of fine buildings in various towns of northern France, in which we have established our field hospitals. In these operations are performed, and very sick men are kept for treatment.

Because of their nearness to the danger line many field hospitals have no women nurses at all. The work of caring for the wounded is done by enlisted men of the medical corps under the direction of ward masters, non-commissioned officers as a general rule. Army surgeons, of course, are in command, and the men receive good care.

Possibly because of the absence of women these field hospitals are apt to be rather bare and unattractive places. Men have complained to me that they had nothing to read. Some said they thought there ought to be a few posters or pictures on the wall. To lie all day staring at a blank expanse of whitewash gets on the nerves of the sensitive. This is, however, a temporary condition. The Library War Service of the American Library Association is now working in France, and every hospital will soon be well supplied with books.

After the evacuation hospital comes the base hospital. Only those cases which promise quick recovery are kept very long near the front. As the war continues those beds will be needed for the freshly wounded, and the chances are that our men wounded in this battle will soon be sent, in fine hospital trains, to the vicinity of Paris, or towns farther south.

I visited an emergency base hospital established and maintained by Johns Hopkins Hospital, and I should be very well satisfied to hear that my son was being cared for there. This hospital is situated in a pleasant wooded spot not many miles from the ancient town which is our general headquarters. It has a main building of brick, an old French country house, but most of the hospital wards are in temporary wooden buildings.

Johns Hopkins itself, with its millions of dollars invested in buildings, has no better equipment than this temporary base hospital in France. It has no better doctors or nurses, and as for its head nurse it has the best head nurse Johns Hopkins ever produced, Miss Bessie Baker.

I know other hospitals, one in a medieval town in central France, several in a pleasant suburb of Paris, and one, perhaps the most picturesque of all, in southern France a few miles from the large seaport which admits many of our ships weekly. This hospital is housed in an old French château that in its garden plan reminded me a little of the White House in Washington. The front garden is small and formal, with a wonderful hedge of white and red camellias. But back of the château the large garden slopes in a series of blossoming terraces down to a great river which flows into the sea a few miles beyond. I can not think of a lovelier or more restful place in which to spend a convalescence.

The quality of nursing in our hospitals overseas is so high that it has excited the admiration of the French and British soldiers. They beg to be sent to "the American hospital." I have heard French officers say that they would be glad to have the entire hospital system in France turned over to the control of the Americans.

The fact is that we have worked out a far gentler system of caring for the wounded, for changing dressings and the like, than any other nation. The British are scientific but Spartan. The French have had few trained nurses until this war. Our nurses are the best in the world.

I shall not fret about my wounded soldier, and I hope other women will make up their minds to bear ordinary bad news from over there with calmness and courage. We can not possibly escape suffering and pain. It is in the world for us to bear, and until the war is won women all over the world must live in a sisterhood of sorrow and anxiety.

When the word comes, "He is wounded," just remember that he is also being taken care of by the most tender and humane means any government in the world ever devised for its soldiers. Even if the dreadful message comes, "Wounded and missing," do not despair. Even that is being looked after by a large department of the Red Cross. Every missing soldier is traced, and if he is found to be a prisoner his needs are provided for—medicine, food, clothing, letters—the Red Cross sees that he gets them promptly.

Besides all its work of relief for sick and wounded soldiers, the Red Cross has a department of medical research which has performed wonders in preventive medicine, and it is still at work, brilliantly and tirelessly, to find ways of fighting pain and death.

# CHAPTER XV
# FIGHTING WOUND SHOCK

"Base Hospital No. ——
"Amex Force, France

"Dear Mother,

"You ought to see your soldier son now! He looks about as military as a smoked ham, and feels like—but my well-known delicacy halts me. Never mind, I'm all here—barring a few pieces of bone that don't matter, and I have gained the honor of having been in the first wave of the first Americans to go over the top at Cantigny.

"Incidentally I have the bullet that hit me, and one boche helmet. I would have got more but my trip was short and sweet—some six hundred yards at most before some unmannerly person slammed me over the knee with a battle-ship, and I sat down to think it over. It struck me suddenly that there was very little of interest to be seen, and it would be a waste of time to go any further.

"From there to where I am now has been a series of more or less painful transfers through first aid posts, dressing stations and French hospitals, with a Red Cross train and a ninety kilometer ride in an ambulance. I don't think you have ever known the joy of a ninety K. ride on the upper deck of a pitching ambulance. It's an experience. I appreciated the sensations of a pup with a tin can tied to his tail.

"But all that is over and I'm settled at last, so far behind the lines that the street lights of the town aren't shaded at all. You must not worry, Mother dear, for I'll be as good as new in three months, and while broken legs are not the sort of thing you go around hunting for, they aren't half as bad as a tooth ache, and mine is a particularly well trained one and doesn't hurt at all."

By the time the news reaches us here in America that one of our beloved has been wounded in France the worst is usually over and the patient is often out of danger. It takes several days for such news to reach Washington and be telegraphed to soldiers' relatives, and if no second telegram comes closely on the first we may be truly thankful.

My son was wounded on the twenty-eighth of May, and it was nearly a month before I heard from him. If this had happened a year ago I should have been paralyzed with fear, not because of the wound, but because of dread of the after effects. One enormous advantage we have over our splendid allies is that we not only benefit from their experience in battle, but from their experience in the hospital. Wounds which for the first three years of the war were impossible to cure are now in the class called favorable.

It is this knowledge that helps to keep me in courage, and I hope it will help all the others. We are too far away to realize the war, but we know that our sons are in deadly peril from German shot and shell.

There has not been enough said about the magnificent work of the army surgeons in restoring men. One of their greatest achievements was the conquest of trench fever. In another chapter I shall tell that story. In this one I shall tell of the great fight they have made—a fight almost if not quite won—against a still more terrible malady, wound shock.

Shock has been called the great mystery of the war. It followed severe wounds, especially those of the abdomen and chest, but frequently it occurred in men only slightly wounded. And it was horribly fatal.

Here was a case: A splendid young man of twenty-three was brought into an advanced dressing station with a foot shot off. Not a fatal wound in ordinary circumstances. But this man who, an hour ago, had been in perfect health, now lay white as marble, cold and almost pulseless. The wounded stump did not even bleed. In a short time he was dead. He was shocked to death.

The best physicians in the world have been working for nearly four years to find out why he, and others, died like that. They were completely baffled at first, but they kept steadily on. They worked in front-line trenches and even on the battle-field trying to understand wound shock.

They undertook extensive and intensive laboratory work to discover the blood changes that took place in men suffering from the strange malady. To a great extent their work has been successful, and the work is triumphantly going on.

The medical research department of the American Red Cross is now conducting a series of experiments, and it might as well be admitted at the outset that these experiments, which are to save men's lives in untold numbers, involve destroying some animal life. For this reason the anti-vivisectionists, and that small section of the press which supports their views, are at the present time hotly assailing the research department of the Red Cross.

Says one statement of the opposition: "No expensively equipped laboratory is needed to seek out wounded soldiers on the battle-fields and give them aid and comfort in the hospitals; and it will cause deep sorrow among innumerable contributors to know that the Red Cross is going beyond the activities of its charter rights and is supporting a cruel and disputed form of medical experimentation."

Putting aside for the moment all except the first sentence of this statement, "No expensively equipped laboratory is needed to seek out wounded soldiers on the battle-fields and give them aid and comfort in the hospitals," the answer is that without the laboratory the hospitals would be back in the days when gunshot wounds were treated by having hot oil poured into them, and when the only way of dealing with shattered limbs was amputation.

This war, particularly, has developed maladies and wound complications undreamed of before. Shock is not exactly new. In civilian hospitals it occurs after every operation. But the wound shock of this war is new, and the doctors had to study it as a new manifestation.

Out of many cases take the following: A soldier member of a working party, laying telephone wires one wet and muddy night, was hit by the explosion of a shell. He was severely wounded, suffering a compound fracture of one arm and some bad muscle lacerations. His comrades picked him up and hurried him to the nearest dressing station, but by the time he got there his wounds looked like dead flesh. There was no bleeding and the man's pulse was still.

He was conscious and mentally bright. "Hello, fellows," he called out to those who worked over him, and to the surgeon he said confidently: "I've got a blighty, haven't I?" Meaning a rest in a home hospital.

Even the surgeon thought so. The case was bad but the man seemed so fit. Yet within an hour he was dead.

There was a sergeant, a hardworking, conscientious man, loved by his fellows. A piece of shell got him as he lay asleep at the foot of a dugout. Both feet were shattered. Within ten minutes the surgeons had the man on the operating table, but he was another case of shock. He died while they were working over him.

Shock has other ways of showing itself. A soldier, very badly wounded in the chest and abdomen, was treated in the advanced dressing station, and as he appeared to be normal in every way he was wrapped up and sent in an ambulance to the evacuation hospital. Within a few hours after he arrived, and when he was sleeping quietly, symptoms of shock appeared.

He sat up in bed struggling and tearing at the bandages which covered his chest. "Air!" he gasped. "I must have air! I can not breathe."

Nurses and doctors surrounded the poor man, trying to alleviate his intense agony. But they knew that this "air hunger," as it is called, was almost certainly a sign of rapidly approaching death.

The doctors had to find out what caused the conditions. They could not tell by simply observing the shocked men. Too many of them died before much observation could be made.

It did not help the doctors to observe that the blood pressure of such patients went down and that most of the blood in their bodies seemed to disappear. Where did it disappear? Nobody knew. The men's pulses stopped, their wounds ceased to bleed. Why? Why did they suffer this awful air hunger? What relation had the low blood pressure to the breathing capacity?

There was one way and one only for them to find out. They had to anesthetize a great many guinea pigs, rabbits and other small animals and subject them while unconscious, to conditions as nearly as possible identical with those under which the men had developed wound shock. Perhaps in future they will find another way. At present that is the only way we have. Following experimentation they examined every organ of the wounded animals, analyzed their blood, minutely studied them, with the result that they know, if not all about wound shock, at least something. They know a great deal about the causes and they are on the track of the cure.

They know, for example, that tremendous changes take place in the system following a battle. The men go into action with their hearts beating abnormally hard and high. They are in a state of intense excitement. When they are wounded there occurs a sharp reaction, both mental and physical, partly because of the wound, partly because of bad conditions which often precede going over the top.

Our men behind the line, even when they are exposed to occasional shell fire, lead almost normal lives. They eat and sleep and keep fairly comfortable, even in bad weather. But in the front trenches, it must be admitted, only the sublime courage and devotion of the men enable them to endure their surroundings with cheerful fortitude.

They have good food in the front trenches, the men have told me. But they are sometimes short of water. They sleep in constantly interrupted snatches. They are wet to the skin and sometimes very cold. They work hard, and are tormented with the noise, the blasting of bullets, the shriek of shells. Often when they go over the top they are tired as dogs, their circulation is sluggish with cold, their bodies are full of waste products.

The mad excitement of battle is followed by the shock of a wound. Icy cold grips them. Their pulses stop. They have wound shock. The doctors now know all this. They have devised, even in the advanced dressing stations, means of keeping wounded men warm in heated blankets over alcohol stoves. The hot tea they give the wounded now contains medicine to counteract the intense acidity of the blood which experiments on animals revealed as a part of shock.

Now, when a poor shocked wounded man struggles with air hunger, the doctors can do something for him. A single injection works a miracle. The struggle ceases immediately. In a few minutes he is asleep. In a few hours he is smoking a cigarette and joking with the man in the next bed. Thousands of lives, perhaps those of your son and my son, have been saved already, because the doctors now know what to do to prevent most wound shocks, and to cure the favorable cases.

Another thing that has killed thousands in this war is an infection called gas gangrene. It is unlike any other gangrene known to the medical world. It is caused by bacteria bred in the mud and filth of the trenches, and by foreign bodies, bits of cloth and the like which contaminate wounds.

But the gangrene does not always confine itself to the wound. A man wounded in the shoulder may first show gangrene in the wound in his arm. A few days later the gangrene may appear in his legs, and he dies. The blood is not contaminated; that has been proved. The gangrene just mysteriously moves around.

The army physicians have got to find out all about this frightful condition, and how to combat it. They can do it only in a laboratory and through animal experimentation. Why should we sentimentalize about it? The animals die, but they suffer little, if at all. Our men suffer most horribly, and all too often they die.

Remember also that when we send our soldiers out into the hell of battle, artillery fire, machine guns, bombs, shrapnel, liquid fire, poison gas, and all the other hideous inventions of German science, we are subjecting them to vivisection of the worst possible kind.

They throw their bodies between the murderous Huns and the rest of the world. Would you save a few thousand or a few million guinea pigs at the expense of the ghastly suffering and death of one of those men? I would not.

# CHAPTER XVI
# HOW THE WAR AGAINST TRENCH FEVER WAS WON

ONE day last January four companies of so-called non-combatant soldiers of the American army in France were lined up to listen to an address from their officers. The men were members of the field hospital and ambulance service. Their officers were army physicians. Working with them were other eminent physicians, members of the medical research department of the American Red Cross. This, or something like it, is what these physicians said to the soldiers:

"Men, we have set ourselves to find out the cause and cure of one of the worst diseases the allied armies have to suffer. It is called trench fever. It is not a fatal disease, but it is slow and painful, and it is so common as to be almost an epidemic. Its ravages are so great that it actually hampers the allies in their struggle to win the war. Something like five hundred thousand men a year are temporarily pulled out of armies because of trench fever.

"The men have to leave the fighting line, go to hospitals and lie there suffering and helpless for weeks on end. One fever does not give positive immunity from others, and it is a fact that many men have recurrent attacks. Trench fever is worst in Flanders, where the British hold the front, but the French, Belgian and Serbian soldiers also suffer from it. When the American army gets here in great numbers we shall undoubtedly see thousands and thousands of our soldiers go under from this disease. Before our men come we want to know what the cause of trench fever is, and how to prevent it.

"We believe that the disease is carried by body lice, but we are not sure. We have tried experiments on animals, guinea pigs and monkeys, but they have not developed the fever. Now we have got to try more experiments, this time on human beings. You remember that the cause of yellow fever was discovered only after brave and devoted men allowed themselves to be bitten by the stegomya mosquito, which was believed to carry the disease. Some of those men died and others were brought to the verge of death. But their deed banished the scourge of yellow fever from the world. Now we are asking for volunteers to help us banish trench fever.

"Men, what we are asking you to do is no easy or agreeable thing. We are asking you to risk a lingering, painful and weakening illness, one that will keep you in bed for five or six weeks and often make you wish you were dead and out of it.

"You will not die, but you will suffer. You will have horrible headaches, pains in your backs, shoulders, knees, abdomens. This disease has been mistaken for appendicitis. It has often been called shinbone fever. This will give you some idea of what trench fever feels like.

"But we are calling for volunteers because we want to prevent any more soldiers from having trench fever. We want to know what causes it, so that we can find out how to prevent it. Fifty or sixty men, willing to suffer these pains once, may prevent millions of men ever again from suffering the same pains. They will do more, they will keep those men in the fighting lines instead of the hospitals, and hence they will importantly help to win the war. We want sixty volunteers. How many have we?"

Four entire companies of field hospital and ambulance soldiers of a certain American division in France were thus appealed to. The entire four companies, as one man, stepped forward and volunteered. Of course they did. That is the kind of soldiers we raised our boys to be.

I saw and talked to some of these men when they were recovering in a hospital near Paris. They were a fine-looking lot of men, American born, all of them, and all but one hailing from the New England states. It just happened so. The division was drafted in the Atlantic states, and these men were selected, regardless of their previous residence, simply because among five or six hundred perfectly fit men they stood out as being in the absolute pink of health and strength.

"We thought," said one of these volunteers to me, "that we were going to be sent up to a front-line trench and sleep in the mud with the cooties till we got it. But to our surprise, they took us up to a perfectly good hospital back of the British lines. Nice clean tents, good beds, and food—um-m! Everything we could ask for."

Even the cooties were clean, in a manner of speaking, for the doctors were taking no chances with their experiment. They sent the eggs of those unpleasant beasts to England, where no trench fever has ever appeared, and when the eggs hatched out they put the beasts on trench fever patients. Then they put them on the volunteers.

About fifty or sixty of the loathsome insects were put on a square of cotton cloth and bound to the forearm of a soldier with strips of adhesive plaster. A piece of surgical cotton over the cloth was well bandaged on, and over the whole dressing a stronger cotton cuff was securely fastened with more adhesive plaster. No possible chance for the insects to escape remained.

Thirty-five soldiers were thus inoculated with trench fever. The rest were reserved for blood inoculation tests. The men who had their arms bound up as described endured an endless biting and chewing from ten to fifteen days until they developed the fever. It was a tormenting ordeal. Their arms became open sores from which blood and pus penetrated the dressings. The first attack of fever and blinding headache must have come as a welcome relief to intolerable itching.

Not a man but that came down with fever. One man ran a high temperature for forty days and nights without a break, but with most of the men the fever and the pain were remittent. Some suffered so severely that the doctors were obliged to inject morphia.

Those men who were inoculated with the blood of the trench fever patients developed the malady almost immediately. They suffered variously with pain and fever, just as the others did.

"The monotony of it was bad," said one of the men, a big teamster from Boston. "Nothin' to do but lay there and burn up and curse the pains in your blasted legs. Next day you'd feel better, perhaps, but so weak that you couldn't move. The nurses were fine, and there was plenty to eat. But we was too sick to care whether there were women around or not, and the best stuff they gave us to eat tasted like sawdust."

They agreed that the monotony of existence in trench fever was worse than the pain. Life was a dreary waste. The eyes of the patients were so affected that they were even denied the solace of reading.

The worst was yet to come for these devoted servants of science. When the German drive began on the twenty-first of last March it was found that their isolation hospital, thought to be so safe, was directly in the line of attack. Lying in their beds, with nothing over them but tent walls, their fever-racked bodies and weakened limbs became tormented by the shriek of shells and the roar of artillery. German airplanes chattered over their heads and bombs exploded around them.

"They wouldn't let us get up and see the show," grumbled one lad in the rest hospital. "Some of us crawled to the door of the tent and saw a little, but those English nurses shooed us back, and when it got hotter they made us dive under the beds. They are dreadful stern, those English nurses. You have to mind them as though they were the doc himself."

By March twenty-seventh the place had got too hot to hold invalids, and the men were taken down to Paris. The journey was a fright. No beds, little food or water, slow trains which took twenty-four hours to traverse a distance of fifty-odd miles; but the men stood it, and when I saw them in the hospital near Paris all but one was out of bed and on the road to health.

They were eating well, and more than one begged me to "use my influence" to get them out of the hospital.

When a sick man begins to eat like a harvest hand and begs to get out it indicates that he has only a few weeks of convalescence ahead of him. At least that is what the head physician of the hospital told me when I put in their petitions.

The cause of trench fever, thanks to our keen army and Red Cross surgeons, and to the courageous men who volunteered to help them, has definitely been established. The trench louse, once called a nuisance, is now known to be almost as dangerous as the stegomya mosquito.

The trench louse must be got rid of, and that, happily, is not a very difficult affair. Our American army authorities will take care of that. And our sons, we may be thankful to know, are going to be spared one of the most frequent and most painful afflictions of the war.

The scientists and physicians who took part in the experiment by which trench fever is to be abolished will receive honors and rewards at the hands of their colleagues and the public. What I would like to know, is what honors and rewards those simple soldiers are going to receive.

# CHAPTER XVII
# THE GREATEST MOTHER IN THE WORLD

JOHN SMITH, of Harlem, gave five dollars to the Red Cross during the last drive. It was a big sum for a man with his responsibilities and a small income to part with, but John gave the money, and all over the country men like him, women, too, and children gave what they could to help the wounded and the desolated across the seas.

I want to tell John and the others how their money was spent, and I shall ask them first to go with me to a huge basement room of the Gare du Nord, the big north station of Paris. The room was taken over by the American Red Cross at the beginning of the spring offensive, March twenty-first, and here for days and nights, terrible days, sinister nights, a stream of refugees from the invalid district poured in and out, coming by train from Soissons, Compiegne, Montdidier, Albert, and from dozens of little villages and farms between Laon and Amiens.

The Red Cross fed and clothed and refreshed these refugees in that basement, loaded them on big motor-trucks and took them across the city to the Orleans or the Quai d'Orsay stations and saw them off to the sheltered south.

All on your money, you fortunate, generous, tender hearted givers. We who were over there in those first desperate days of spring had the privilege only of helping the Red Cross take care of the stricken men, women and children who had fled before the German hordes for the second time since the war began.

Vividly before me I see that great basement room, the only kind of a place that is half-way safe in Paris these days. It is night, or, rather, it is early morning, nearly two o'clock, and I have spent every minute of the time since nine o'clock fitting shoes, your gift, to refugee children.

When I went on duty early in the evening there were five or six babies standing at the counter, over the edge of which their little white, dirty, tired faces were barely visible, and their round black eyes were fixed enviously on a huge pile of shoes waiting to be distributed.

I picked up the smallest babe, a little boy of four, and asked him if he needed shoes. "*Oui*, madame," he did, and stockings, too, for his feet were literally on the ground. I grabbed a bunch of stockings, found the right size, and explored that great pile of shoes until that infant was fitted, and then I attended to the rest, for all those children needed both shoes and stockings.

So, it appeared to me that night, did almost every child in France. They came on and on, some in their mother's arms, some toddling along, some leading other children. I worked steadily, with only a pause now and then when a new trainload came in and were fed.

The shoes were new and they rubbed off, and soon my hands and face and big gingham apron were streaked and spotted with black. I was almost as dirty as the refugees, but still the children demanded shoes.

They forgot that they had endured agonies of fear and horror, they forgot the roar of the shells in the village streets. They forgot the hunger and thirst and the deadly weariness of the flight. Their little stomachs were full, they were warm and safe, and they had new stockings and new shoes on their feet.

They had more, for when my part was done other women took them in hand and gave them new shirts and gowns and the shiny black pinafores which every French child, boy as well as girl, looks upon as an indispensable article of dress. If you could have seen their smiles, heard their lisping words of gratitude, felt their warm little handclasps, oh, you fortunate and generous givers, you would have been repaid a thousand, thousand times for your gift to the Red Cross.

Because the French rarely have large families, it must not be thought that they do not value children. They adore children, as a matter of fact, and their gratitude to the Red Cross for what was done for children during those days of flight and anguish was pathetic to see and hear.

Women came into the basement of the Gare du Nord in a condition of half nudity. When the storm burst they gathered up their babies, took what they could carry of household goods and treasures, and simply fled. Much of what they carried was lost by the wayside. Their clothes were rags. Some of the rags were taken off by the mothers that the children might be kept alive, for the weather was cold and rainy. But when these poor women came into the Red Cross room their first thought was always for their babies.

"You have need of shoes yourself, madame," I said to more than one. She always answered, "Yes, but *le petit* first."

When you saw a woman who would not eat, who cared not at all for the new blouse or the warm coat they offered her, who wept unceasingly or wore a look of wild misery like insanity, you knew that she had lost her children in the flight. That happened not infrequently. Part of the money you gave the Red Cross is spent to find those lost children and bring them back to the desolate mother's breast.

Late one night during that exciting period in March the workers at the Gare du Nord found a boy of thirteen who had been separated early in the flight from his family. He had walked a distance of twenty kilometers, twelve and a half miles, before he reached the railroad station, and he carried with him on that walk, and on the journey to Paris, two bags of feed for the horse, four or five pounds of beans in a paper sack, a cross-cut saw, two axes, some harness and a gas mask. When the Red Cross workers discovered him he was about all in, but he was brave. He sat on his baggage and ate sandwiches and drank hot chocolate like a famished tramp.

He had an aunt and a grandmother in Paris, he said, but he did not know his aunt's married name. He knew the name of the street she lived on, though, and the next morning a Red Cross man went with the boy to the street, and by simple process of calling at every house in every block finally located the aunt.

But that wasn't all. Eloi, his name was Eloi Beaussart, needed a job, and the Red Cross gave it to him. Now that game youngster wears a khaki uniform with A. R. C. on the collar, and works in a Red Cross canteen. When I came away Eloi's family had not yet been found, but he was serene and hopeful. The American Red Cross, in his opinion, can do anything if you give it time.

Your money did not wait until the refugees got to Paris before it helped them. In front of the Red Cross headquarters in the Place de la Concorde crowds gathered daily to see the great motor-trucks being loaded with food to be sent up into the fringes of the war zone. Thousands of loaves of bread, tins of meat, condensed milk, chocolate, coffee, everything necessary and practical.

The Red Cross had a great many stations in the sections over which the Germans swept, and while the workers in those stations were helping to evacuate whole populations, the workers in Paris were rushing supplies to feed them. With guns roaring and shrapnel bursting around them, the Red Cross camions went steadily on taking hope and relief and life to thousands of civilians and wounded soldiers.

In one station yard, waiting for trains to carry them to base hospitals down the line, the Red Cross found and succored three thousand wounded French soldiers. In the town of Beauvais, almost the last habitable point near the war zone, a large number of sick civilians, mostly women and children, were found. There was no hospital left in the place, which had been shelled and largely evacuated, and to show you how promptly your money acts, I am going to tell you what the Red Cross workers did for the suffering population of Beauvais.

Some time in the early morning a hospital was established on paper. That is, it was decided to establish a hospital. At ten o'clock that same morning a partially furnished house was rented. At twelve o'clock the house was in order, a surgery with full supplies was installed, two doctors, four nurses and several helpers were at their posts, and before the afternoon was half over forty patients were in the beds and being treated and cared for.

Wouldn't you rather feel that you had helped do a job like that than to have another summer hat?

In the quaint old city of Toul, through which the famous Rhine-Marne canal flows, and close to which our troops first held the line against the Germans, I saw another hospital, a children's hospital established and supported by Red Cross money. The four hundred and sixty-six little children in this place came from towns and villages which have been bombarded with gas bombs, instruments of torture invented in hell especially for the German army.

Those bombs killed, suffocated to death, a large number of babies, but the Red Cross rescued many. There in that hospital on the hill above Toul four hundred and sixty-six children have had their tortured lungs cleared of the poisonous stuff, and their anguished little bodies have been brought back to ease.

Wouldn't you be happier helping a gassed French child back to life than to buy a box of expensive cigars?

There is not room enough in one chapter or in a dozen of them, to tell half of what the Red Cross has done and is doing in France alone in this war.

Twenty-three hundred people, doctors, nurses, canteen workers, business men, social workers and others are enrolled in France. Twenty hospitals, seventy-six dispensaries and several sanitariums are in operation. For wounded soldiers of the allies the Red Cross supplies nearly four thousand hospitals. It has a model hospital train; it has innumerable dressing stations, canteens, health stations, sewing rooms for the destitute. Nearly three million soldiers a month are served in Red Cross canteens alone.

In Paris there are thirteen canteens always busy serving French soldiers on leave. In Bourg there is a canteen where thousands of our soldiers going to Aix-les-Bains and Chambéry for their vacations got a real American home breakfast. I heard many soldiers speak enthusiastically of that breakfast, served by the Red Cross women, but purchased by mothers, fathers and friends of American soldiers right here in the United States.

Those sons of ours who are being rapidly transported to France to join the more than a million already there soon will be training behind the battle lines in Lorraine, Picardy, the Aisne. Soon after that they will be fighting, the fight to death if need be, to clear the world of that evil thing, war.

Between them and such suffering as no one who has not seen it can even faintly imagine stands that cross of mercy and devotion. To support it is to support and protect our own children. "Give till it hurts," I read on one of the Red Cross posters. Give, if you have hearts, until your hearts stop hurting.

---

# CHAPTER XVIII
# FRANCE APPROVES THE EGREC EM SAY AH

THE Y. M. C. A. has started a new drive both for money and for workers. John R. Mott, general secretary of the National War Work Council of the Association, has announced that they must recruit four thousand new workers for France and Italy, and of course they must have money to support the work already going and that to be started soon.

The exact sum has not yet been announced, but whatever it is the people of this country will give it. To give to the Y. M. C. A. is to contribute directly to the comfort, happiness, and, to a very great extent, the safety of our own enlisted men in France. I have been in dozens of Y. M. C. A. huts and canteens, and I say emphatically that our army could hardly maintain its highest efficiency without these places. They are the nearest substitutes for homes that were ever devised for any army.

When troops are quartered in an interesting old French city, as some of our troops are, there are many things in which the soldier off duty can interest himself. But the vast majority of American soldiers are not quartered in cities or even in towns. They are in camps differing very little from the training camps at home. Or else they are billeted in villages. In that case they sleep in barns or in peasant cottages. When they are off duty there is not a blessed thing for them to do except walk up and down the muddy streets and talk.

Those French villages of the north, especially in winter, are picturesque in the extreme when viewed from a motor-car, but as a place of residence they leave much to be desired. A stranger might have some difficulty in distinguishing between the houses and the barns, the huge manure heaps, which are the chief wealth of the owners, being about equally distributed before all the buildings. I have seen scores of these little hamlets, with their signs on each door, giving the number of officers, men or horses billeted within, and I have sometimes wondered by what process the authorities decided which buildings were for *hommes* and which for *chevaux*. Those are the first two French words our soldiers learn over there.

But wherever our soldiers are quartered, they must have a Y. M. C. A. hut. They can not get along without it. It serves as a club, a night school, a shop, a library, a theater, lecture room, movie, gymnasium, writing-room. It is a great place in which to get acquainted with French people, for next to the Red Cross the Y. M. C. A. is the most admired of all American institutions with which the French have come in contact.

They pronounce it *"Egrec, Em, Say, Ah,"* and most of them have not the slightest idea of what the letters mean, but they highly approve of the thing itself. In the towns and cities they flock to the Y. M. C. A. entertainments, especially the military band concerts. There is very little music in France just now, aside from our bands.

The Y. M. C. A. hut and canteen does its greatest work in the isolated camps where the soldiers are cut off from all other recreation. I remember a hut in one of our largest aviation camps, miles away from any town or village. Life in an aviation camp is something like working in a planing mill. The sound of hundreds of aeroplane motors goes on in a ceaseless clatter for hours every day. There is always a strong wind blowing because aviation camps are located on the biggest, emptiest treeless plains that can be found.

The particular aviation camp of which I write was on the widest, flattest plain in France, I should think. There were not nearly enough machines there when I visited it in early April, and the men had very little to do. Hundreds of our flyers in France have never had a chance to do any flying at all, and in this camp, as they said, "If a fellow got a hop once a week he was lucky."

What those boys would have done without their Y. M. C. A. hut I can not imagine. The secretary had been a professor of mathematics in a college somewhere. He was a middle aged, intellectual, rather shy man, and at first I wondered why he had been appointed to such a post. But when I saw him in a crowd of soldiers I no longer wondered. He was easy, genial, sympathetic, tactful, what the politicians call a perfect mixer. When he stood up to introduce the speaker of the evening the boys stamped their feet and whistled through their fingers like kids.

"How will you ever go back to teaching mathematics after this?" I asked him.

"I never will go back," he replied. "I'm going to be human for the rest of my life."

He was being human in that camp so successfully that he almost succeeded in offsetting the lack of planes. At least, he did wonders in keeping alive the spirit of courage and hopefulness among the men.

A dozen miles or so from a large southern seaport where many thousands of our men are at work I visited another Y. M. C. A. place, one which has become the social center of an entire French town. In the big town there is a flourishing Y. M. C. A., and when the building camps began to string along the river harbor for miles the secretary in charge saw that extension of the work would have to be made.

He picked from his staff a remarkable young Vassar girl who speaks good French and asked her if she would go down to a certain small town, the central point of half a dozen camps, and establish a Y. M. C. A. headquarters. She went. She found on the main street, which is also the river front, an old inn where business was getting duller every day, and she rented it. There was no electric light in the house, and the plumbing was early Victorian.

Within a week the house was scrubbed from top to bottom and freshly papered and painted. Within a few more weeks it was wired for electric lights, it had shower baths for soldiers and the only bathroom in the entire town. There was a canteen where six hundred men a day could get a sit-down meal of very good food and a counter where many more could buy chocolates and cigarettes. There was a writing- and reading-room, a room where French lessons were furnished, another where boxing and wrestling matches could be held. There was a piano and a phonograph, and a little way down the street there was a large hall for entertainments.

By this time Miss Christy had asked for and was given an assistant, another live wire of a young woman. They soon had three or four French women for cooks and assistants, and they were doing a land office business. When I visited them the entire house was so full of soldiers that the two secretaries were deploring the fact that they had not twice the room, especially for canteen purposes.

Everybody in town uses that headquarters. The mayor goes there to take a bath. Officers from the camps visit it almost as often as the men.

These are two samples only. All the Y. M. C. A. headquarters are doing good work. These two were notable because of the personality of the secretaries, which was above the average. There are many such working for the Y. M. C. A. There were half a dozen at Aix-les-Bains, where our men went for vacation leaves. Some of them had prominent names as well. Mrs. Theodore Roosevelt, Jr., was on the staff at the Aix casino. Her tireless work, her frank and democratic manners delighted the men. "She works, too," they said admiringly.

In another Y. M. C. A. canteen I saw young Mrs. Vincent Astor on duty. She walked up and down between the tables anxiously observing whether Private Bill Snyder, of Lancaster, Pennsylvania, and Corporal Joe Morgan, of Weeping Water, Nebraska, got pie where pie was due, or an extra helping of jam where requested. Associated with Mrs. Astor was Ethel Harriman, now the wife of a lieutenant in the army.

The Y. M. C. A. wants more of those women, not because they are rich and "fashionable," but because they have social experience, good manners, tact, agreeable qualities. There is no room in the world now for what used to be called society women. The place for leisure class women is nursing sick and wounded soldiers and helping to serve and to entertain well ones. The Y. M. C. A. wants at least eight hundred more women. It wants business women, executive women, talented women. It ought to get the eight hundred and a big reserve as well.

Of course, the Y. M. C. A. will get all the money it needs, and that without any controversy. Never mind if it has made mistakes. We can criticize the mistakes after we have given the money. And right here let me say that one of the head men in the Paris executive headquarters told me that the Y. M. C. A. was hard at work rectifying some of the mistakes they made in the beginning, and which were absolutely inevitable in the face of unknown conditions and unforseen problems.

"We know now," said this man, "that it was a grave mistake to send over men of draft age. We shall not do that in future. We know that we have some useless timber over here, and we are going to weed it out. We know that a religious man, one who can lead in prayer and preach a good sermon, is not necessarily a good executive secretary in a war region. We are finding that out. We know that not all the women we have brought over here have made good. We will replace them. Just give us time."

I have heard it mentioned as a mistake of the Y. M. C. A. that the leaders do not force prayer meetings on the men, that it has given up some of its religious quality. In my opinion, the Y. M. C. A. is much more religious now than it ever was before in all its history. It lives its religion every hour of the day, and it has learned a beautiful religious tolerance. To Protestant and Catholic, Jew and Gentile alike it gives the same generous and never failing love and charity.

To me it is an evidence of the true religious spirit that in Y. M. C. A. huts you may see displayed a notice that Father Maguire will hear confessions of Catholic soldiers on Saturday in such and such a room. Or that a Sedar service for Jewish soldiers will be held on such a date at the following addresses. It is the only kind of religion that appeals to me. It is the only kind I ever heard that the founder of Christianity preached. It is the strongest possible reason why we should give money, all that is asked for, to the Y. M. C. A.

# CHAPTER XIX
# BEAUTY AS USUAL

BEFORE the war there were few European peoples of whom we knew less, whom we misunderstood as thoroughly, as the French. We had a French tradition in the United States once, but that was long ago. New Orleans, St. Louis, and Charleston, South Carolina, were to a certain extent French cities up to the time of the Civil War. Old family names, the names of streets and squares, even a few monuments bear witness to this. But even in New Orleans the French tradition is now only a shadow. We have had little immigration from France in late years. Hence we know little of the people. There was a vague theory that they were frivolous, pleasure-loving and rather lax in their morals.

The French are not frivolous—they are volatile and gay. They are not pleasure-loving, any more than other peoples are. The questionable pleasures of Paris, the bal masques and the Moulin Rouge sort of thing, existed for tourists mainly. We thought the French liked that kind of unwholesome painted stuff because it was there, and they thought we liked it because we paid almost anything to get it. It is time the two people, French and Americans, understood each other.

I think I can not convey a better idea of the French character, its unquestionable gaiety and indomitable courage, than by telling how through all risks and dangers and calamities, their worship of pure beauty persists. Beauty is a cult with the French. They can not endure anything ugly. Every national emotion is expressed in terms of beauty and grace.

Paris, as we know, has been under bombardment from the German long-distance guns since March twenty-third. Almost every day the gun has sounded. Some days its spiteful boom sounded every fifteen minutes from dawn until dark. Now one of the effects of this constant bombardment was that it threatened to break all the expensive plate-glass windows in the capital, and the people were advised to paste strips of paper across their windows. Window glass just now is not only expensive, but it is very scarce. Once broken, replacement becomes a serious matter.

Of course, strips of paper can not stop a shell or a piece of shrapnel, but they can lessen the shock of concussion. So Paris overnight blossomed from one end to the other with paper-stripped window glass.

But did they just paste on strips of paper, as almost any other people in the world would have done? They did not. They invented a new art of window decoration. Every merchant, every householder, vied with all the others to make their striped-up windows things of beauty. They devised color schemes, they studied historic design, they made the paper strips advertise wares. In a word, bombs might fall, but beauty went on as usual.

But the most extraordinary manifestation of the unquenchable spirit of the French was the discussion, immediately opened, as to what a properly self-respecting woman, awakened in the night by death-dealing bombs from the sky, ought to wear when she fled to the cellar.

A leading Paris newspaper featured an interview with a well-known dressmaker in which the subject was thoroughly threshed out. The dressmaker recalled the fact that during the Reign of Terror of the French revolution the doomed aristocrats dressed for the guillotine as for a function, this being their last defiance of the mob. Hence it was but proper that their descendants, the French women of to-day, should not permit the German terror to interfere with their duty to look well on all occasions.

This *couturière* did not have to urge this duty on her clients. They overwhelmed her, she declared, with demands. It had become for them necessary to make frequent descents to the bowels of the earth, and that suddenly. What were they to put on? Nothing in their wardrobe seemed either suitable or practical.

Thus pressed, madame proceeded to invent a cellar gown. It sounds funny, but, after all, it may not be. Remember that the Parisians often had to leave their houses and walk or run half a block or so to find adequate shelter from aerial bombs. Hence a warm garment was called for. A woman is not necessarily robed for the street and for a damp cellar, twenty feet underground, when she throws a kimono over her nightgown. No!

"It was no small problem, you can readily understand," declared madame. "I was obliged to invent a gown that one could put on quickly, at the first sound of the *alerte*. After much thought I decided on a domino model. By its simplicity and the amplitude of its dimensions, it is well suited to a rapid adjustment and a quick flight. It is provided with an ample hood to cover the hair and to guard against cold draughts.

"The traditional domino, however, is not provided with any pockets. These, of course, are very necessary in present conditions, since a number of indispensable objects accompany, or should accompany, a lady to a cave. She wishes to take with her not only the most precious of her jewels and *bijoux*, but her purse, watch, keys, mirror, also divers other small objects; an electric torch, manicuring tools, a box of powder, a lip stick, perhaps.

"She will require a pencil and a pad of paper, in case she wishes to keep a diary of events. She may wish to carry with her certain photographs which she can not bear to lose. Certainly she will need some morsels of chocolate, and in case the raid is a prolonged one, something to read. My bombardment robe contains pockets enough and ample for all emergency requirements."

The color of the bombardment robe, or cellar gown, was an important item. The average cave *abri* or cellar is not noted for its spotlessness. One must look out for that. Hence the proper color of the gown was something practical—brown, gray or taupe. However, the inventor of the gown found no ordinary color exactly to her mind.

She did not wish one of her clients, in the semi-obscurity of a cave, to be mistaken for a sack of potatoes, nor yet to be trodden on by an excited new arrival. She sought a color which should be neutral and yet outstanding, and she found it in a tint she called "*chaudron*," the identification of which I shall have to leave to the experts.

It must be a very nice color, however. If you should have to hide in a coal cellar, it was said, the contact with the coal will not injure your appearance, but will paint your cellar gown with lovely Rembrandt effects. Moreover, the hood of this *robe au chaudron* is lined with some soft, tender color, which will lend beauty to the countenance of the wearer, and presumably make the cold and discomfort easier to endure.

I never descended to the caves during the air raid, preferring to take my chances on a lower floor. But if I did feel constrained to seek a wine cave, or a coal cellar while boche bombs were hurtling through the atmosphere, I admit I might like to wear something becoming. Anyhow, as long as the French go on making their lives beautiful in spite of air raids and guns that shoot seventy miles, in spite of devastating German hordes in the north and a war that shows small signs of abating, I think they prove themselves bad to beat, and allies we ought to be proud to claim.

Another thing I admired in the French was their constant sense of humor. They laughed at the Germans. The big gun, full of hate as it was, furnished a subject of jest.

The cartoonist drew caricatures of it that were full of wit. When one of the guns burst, killing, as it must have, a number of German gunners, a cartoonist pictured the inventor pointing to a miscellaneous collection of arms and legs which decorated the landscape, saying proudly: "You see, super-colonel, how kolossaly powerful my kanon is. It is as deadly at one end as it is at the other!" The Parisians found this irresistibly comic.

They laughed scornfully at the solemn lies published in the German papers regarding the alleged panic their bombardment was creating. I have seen men and women sitting outside the cafés in the Rue Royale and on the boulevards, sipping their *apéritifs* before dinner and enjoying these exaggerations, as reprinted in the Paris papers.

They smiled and chuckled over the news announced in the Stuttgart *Neues Tageblatt* that Paris would soon be a mass of ruins; that even the working class population no longer had the hardihood to remain. The roads leading to Tours, Orleans, Lyons, cities of the south, were crowded with interminable convoys, vehicles drawn by horses, donkeys and even dogs. Sick women were being transported in baby carriages. The forest of Fontainbleau was one vast camp of refugees.

"Listen then to this, *mon vieux*," reads a highly diverted Frenchman to his neighbor at the next table. "It is not only from fear of the Germans that the entire population is in flight, but it is from fear of the French themselves. The capital is filled with deserting soldiers and other disaffected persons who wait only a favorable opportunity to overthrow the government. Do you hear? The *Berliner Tageblatt* says so."

Funniest of all to the Parisians were the tales of how the whole of Paris not fleeing to the south was living day and night underground, and how not only people but all public monuments were being sent to the caves.

A cartoon in *Le Matin*, I think it was, represented a Frenchman remarking to a friend that the fog was so thick yesterday that he couldn't see the Eiffel Tower. "Oh, haven't you heard?" exclaims the other, "Clemenceau has hidden it in the Metro."

I write this also to give the American people an idea of the fantastic "news" with which the Germans feed their people and keep alive in them the hope that they can ultimately win this war. Some of these German dispatches appear in our own newspapers, exaggerated accounts of victories, absurd estimates of damage inflicted by bombardments. We should laugh at them as the French do.

The Germans tell their hungry populations that terror is winning the war, that the French civil population is in flight and that the government is tottering. It is ridiculously untrue. Many people have left Paris, just as our people would seek refuge from a like situation.

All the people who have summer homes have gone to them earlier than usual. There is a systematic movement to take as many children as possible outside the danger zone. Delicate women and invalids have generally gone. That is all.

# CHAPTER XX
# BLED WHITE

MR. HOOVER tells us that we must save more food. Especially more wheat. With all the sacrifices we have voluntarily made, with all the ingenuity women have used to save food and still keep their families well nourished, the women are called upon to do more. As far as wheat and a few other staples are concerned, Mr. Hoover tells us that our shipments abroad are only now beginning to approach the "minimum requirements" of our soldiers and of our allies.

I know that many housewives the country over will read this announcement with dismay, and will wonder how much more will be required of them, and how much more they can contrive to give. I want to say to the housekeepers who read this, that they can not possibly know or dream the vast importance of their part in this war. They can not know what their food conservation efforts have meant to the French people, as well as the English, the Italians, and what is left of the stricken Belgians.

Every woman who has conscientiously observed the food regulations, thereby releasing food for our soldiers and the allies, has almost literally fought side by side with the men. She has stood by them and fed them, encouraged them, given them physical and spiritual power to go on, wholeheartedly, in the fight for civilization.

A soldier who goes into battle half nourished, one whose heart is heavy thinking of hungry children at home, is a soldier half beaten. He who goes forward with a well-nourished body and a mind at rest is a soldier three-quarters victorious.

This is how you have helped fight the battle for the peace of the world, women of America. And let me assure you that Europe is fully awake to the fact. Nothing that President Wilson has done, or Congress, or the men at the head of our wonderful army in France, has made a deeper impression on the allies than what the housekeepers of this country have done.

Without any compulsion, without any laws, simply because they were appealed to in the name of humanity, hundreds of thousands of women, rich and poor, in great houses and in farm kitchens, have voluntarily rearranged their whole scale of living, have divided up their food with people they will never know nor see.

It has captured the hearts of the people of Europe. They are lost in admiration. It has taught them what they never believed before—that the United States, far from being the land of the dollar, is a land of idealists.

This was precisely the kind of encouragement our allies in Europe needed. They needed it as much as they needed guns, airplanes, soldiers. It was at a very dark hour in the history of this war that the United States entered the war.

I do not mean that our allies were at the breaking point. But they were near the point of desperation because of the sudden and unexpected defection of Russia. The immediate future was heavy with dread.

Then came the news, "the Yanks are coming." The black cloud was lifted. The world was saved. Everybody knows the difficulties that had to be overcome before an American army was landed in France. Germany did not believe that we could land an army there, but we did.

And long before that we landed enough food in France, and in other hungry lands overseas, to enable the allies to carry on until our men came. That was one of the big feats of the war, and in it the women played their part, and more than their part.

No one has had to call for a congressional investigation into the women's share in the war. Because the men who are in the training camps, on the seas and in the fighting zone are not soldiers to us. They are our sons. The French and English soldiers, the Canadians, the men from Australia, South Africa, Italy, Belgium, they too, are mothers' sons, and we don't go back on our sons.

What the mothers of this country have done for the men who fight, and for their people at home, has been to bring hope to their hearts and laughter to their lips. It has enabled them to face danger with a smile.

Every once in a while since I returned from France I have heard the phrase, "The English and the French are bled white." Don't you believe it. After nearly four years of appalling carnage, after the loss of millions of their best and bravest, the courage of our allies, men and women, is marvelous. Since we came into the war that courage has become exaltation. Nothing can shake it.

For all that we have been able to do in the way of supplying the allies with food, it will not do to assume that they have more than enough to keep themselves in good condition. The English seem to have a greater shortage than the French, but that is mainly, I think, because the French know better how to prepare and serve food, and how to make a simple meal attractive.

In England I often felt not exactly hungry but a dissatisfaction which was almost as bad. The diet was monotonous. Meat was almost invariably roasted, vegetables were always boiled and served without sauces.

In France, on the other hand, they have made an art of dining, and even now, in war time, they give you the impression that you are being extremely well fed. Yet the French are short of breadstuffs. Their war bread is good, and I had enough of it at every meal. But the average person in France eats twice and three times the amount of bread at a meal that is eaten in America. Bread is literally the staff of life in France.

Meat, while expensive, was plentiful all during the winter. That was because there was so little grain. They could not afford to feed their cattle and so slaughtered them. Beginning May fifteenth the French food authorities decreed three meatless days a week for the republic, and since France is generally Catholic, that meant for the majority four days, an additional day, Friday, being observed by the Catholics.

There was milk for little children and for invalids, but, except for a small jug with my morning coffee, I never saw milk while I was in France. Butter could be used in limited quantities in cooking, but it was forbidden to be served at the table.

Sugar, too, was almost a forbidden article. Some hotels and private houses served a little sugar with coffee and tea, but mostly the saccharine substitute was offered. Just before I left France, at the end of April, sugar cards were being issued entitling the holders to a pound of white sugar each month.

Only plain bread is baked in France. The innumerable little rolls and crescents, so delicious with the morning coffee, have disappeared. There is no such thing as pastry. Sweets are supplied in jams and marmalades, a limited quantity being allowed once or twice a day. There are no desserts except fruits, fresh or preserved.

I go into this that the American housekeepers who read these articles may see how cheerfully the allies are bearing what our people would consider a real food shortage. They have enough over there, and will have as long as we give of our store, but we are not by any means supporting our allies in luxury. On what they have, however, they live and keep up a spirit that is truly marvelous.

One evening in my London hotel I sat down to dinner near a table where five young people, evidently brothers and sisters, were quietly making merry. One of the men was in the uniform of the Royal Flying Corps, the other, although of military bearing, was in the correct evening clothes of the British civilian.

I noticed that the girl sitting next the man in evening clothes was assiduous in her attentions to him, and it occurred to me that English women too often spoiled their brothers, made them selfish. This golden-haired English girl cut up her brother's food, even fed it to him. I thought it a little absurd.

But when they rose from the table I saw with a shock that the splendid young man had had both arms cut off below the elbows. He probably had been an artillerist. At all events here he was, a helpless cripple. But from the gay demeanor of that family no one would have dreamed that they had a care in the world. They were carrying on, they would have told you.

I saw more of the French than of the English; therefore I saw more instances of their incomparable courage in the midst of war and carnage. I was in Paris when the long-distance gun of the Germans began to bombard the city.

Every fifteen minutes "boom" went the gun, and you held your breath wondering where the shell had fallen and how many people it had killed and wounded.

It was nerve-racking, there is no use denying the fact. In a battle the shells come tearing through the sky, screeching and whining as they come. But in such a long-distance bombardment there are no preliminary sounds. A house explodes before your eyes, the pavement rises up in a geyser of earth and stones, the earth of a park or public garden suddenly flies up in a huge, fan-shaped eruption of smoke and dirt.

Afterward you hear the BOOM! It seems incredible that only three or four minutes ago men in gray-green uniforms, seventy miles away in Germany, loaded that gun, pulled a string or lever or whatever they do pull, and started that shell toward Paris.

It seems impossible to believe that while you stand there wondering, those same men are loading the big gun to again bombard an open town, full of women and children, regardless of where the shell falls.

One Sunday afternoon, just before I came away, I went down into the island of the old city, the original Paris, to say good-by to certain beautiful things I love. It was a lovely spring day and the quay of flowers and the Palace quay were crowded with Parisians out for a Sunday walk. The women wore their spring finery, and there were many little girls in shining white dresses and veils of their first communion.

The long-distance gun had been silent for about forty hours. It gets out of order easily, or else the allied airmen had been shelling it. Anyhow, it had been silent. But suddenly, about fifty yards from where I stood, the waters of the Seine shot up in a great waterspout, there was an explosion and the usual BOOM. A shell had skimmed over the heads of that Sunday crowd of inoffensive Parisians and landed in the river. In a minute the surface of the water was sprinkled with dead fish.

Of course, the object of this bombardment is to frighten and discourage the French. Let me tell you how far it falls short of its object. The cables no doubt carried the story of one shot from that long-distance gun that struck a maternity hospital, killing in their beds mothers and new-born babies. A nurse was killed also, and many women were wounded. The hospital ward itself was reduced to matchwood. It was a horrible thing.

In the midst of all this horror, and as a result of it, a young woman was prematurely delivered of a child, a little girl. The mother died, but the little baby girl lived, and the nurses called in a priest and had that baby christened Victory.

One day, through the streets of Paris they were hauling a captured German cannon, one of the number which now reposes in the courtyard of the Hotel des Invalides. The people stopped to watch the cannon go by, but there was no demonstration of hatred.

The French respect an honorable foe; it is only unclean warfare that they scorn. This was demonstrated right then and there, for as the cannon passed on "Big Bertha," as they call the long-distance gun, suddenly spoke, and somewhere a shell fell in Paris.

A workman in a white smock raised his fist and bawled out in the direction of the German frontier: "That's right, bark, you cur. This one can no longer bite!"

# CHAPTER XXI
# THE REPATRIATES

EVIAN-LES-BAINS is a charming little French town situated near the Swiss frontier. Before the war Evian was a health resort, rivaling Aix-les-Bains, farther south, in its stimulating climate and its medicinal baths. It was a place where the rich and the comfortably circumstanced of almost every country in Europe went to regain lost health. Now it is a place where some of the most miserable people in all the world may be seen. For Evian is the place where Germany returns to France those French men, women and children who are no longer of any use as prisoners and slaves.

They are mostly the people who were taken in the first victorious rush of the Germans in 1914. As long as they could work, or by threats and cruelty could be induced to try to work, the Germans held them as industrial slaves. When, through starvation, exhaustion and disease, they became useless to their taskmasters they were returned to France.

I do not know at what rate these victims of Germany's ambition and lust for world power are now coming back, but last autumn and winter, when the migration was at its height, the repatriates were being received and cared for at the rate of five hundred to one thousand a day. They came through Switzerland, a three days' journey, in rough box cars, often without food or water, and were nearly always, when they arrived, in a condition bordering on collapse.

I want to tell about some of these French repatriates. I shall not exaggerate or embroider the tale. It hurts cruelly to remember those poor people. It hurts to write about them. But I want our people to know. The next time they sit in a meeting where disloyal so-called socialists warble their phrases about this struggle being a profiteers' war, about peace by negotiations, and the rest of it, perhaps they will remember.

The French government created a commission to handle the stream of human derelicts which Germany sent back through Switzerland. The people of Evian lent wholehearted aid to the commission, and all efforts have been splendidly augmented by the American Red Cross.

When the trains came in at the receiving station at Evian there were always a certain number of the returned prisoners who had to be taken immediately to the hospital. They were in advanced stages of tuberculosis, they were suffering from anemia and starvation and from all the diseases of neglect. Worst of all, many women and children were found suffering from the diseases of vice and crime.

All these sick ones go to hospitals. The American Red Cross established a children's hospital at Evian, since nearly sixty per cent. of the repatriates are children, and nearly all of them need hospital care. The French have their local hospitals, and also what they call houses of repose where those of their countrymen not actually sick but extremely exhausted are cared for and put into condition to travel farther.

The emaciated, hollow-eyed and weary remnant who could walk that far are, or were, taken to the old casino, where wealth and fashion used to gather for bridge and expensive food and drink. There the mayor of Evian made a touching speech welcoming the people back to their native land, comforting and cheering them as well as he could. Then they sat down to the first good meal they had eaten, some of them, for years. But first *The Marseillaise* was sung.

"Arise, children of the land,

The day of glory has arrived."

Who could listen, without deep stirrings of emotion, to men and women just released from prison-houses of pain and horror singing those words? I can not imagine how they found voices to sing. Some of them, indeed, could not sing. They could hardly speak. They just stood there dumb and broken, their sad eyes streaming with tears. Even freedom and the sound again of their beloved French language could not wipe out their terrible memories.

Some of the repatriates are met at Evian by friends and relatives. Some are cared for by the French government, sent to towns and villages well away from the war zone. Charity and the Red Cross have done splendid work for all refugees, but their problems are often almost unsolvable. Hardly a man among them is fit for industry. As for the women, the plight of many of them is pitiable.

The individual stories of some of these women I heard from the lips of a woman known throughout France for her devoted labors in behalf of victims of German soldiers in the invaded districts.

This noble French woman bears the beautiful name of Avril de Ste. Croix. I mention it not because she would particularly care to have me do so, but because she is known to a great many women in America. Madame Avril de Ste. Croix is president of the French National Council of Women, and as a prominent suffragist has attended a number of meetings of the International Association for Woman Suffrage of which an American woman, Carrie Chapman Catt, is president. Every one in France and in the United States who knows Madame de Ste. Croix knows that she is incapable of misstatement or misrepresentation. What she told me I am absolutely confident was true in every particular.

In Paris there is a house of mercy established and maintained by patriotic and generous French people for the rehabilitation of women and girl victims of German lust, and Madame de Ste. Croix is managing director of the establishment.

To this house was brought, about a year ago, a woman who, at the beginning of the war, lived with her husband and five children in one of the French cities taken by the Germans. They did not destroy this city, but occupied it and made it a division headquarters.

Madame Doran we will call her, because it is not her name, lost her husband's protection and a good deal of her income at the mobilization. The husband joined the colors, and the wife and five children made a home in two small rooms of a tenement. The whole town was filled with German soldiers, and Madame Doran had two men billeted on her. She moved her family into one room and gave the other to the soldiers.

From the first these soldiers tried to debauch the poor woman. She successfully resisted them. They moved on and two more soldiers were billeted on her. They in turn attempted the degradation of this decent wife and mother. She resisted these men also.

For a year and a half she lived with her children in that room, separated only by a thin wall from lustful brutes whose orders were that "the German seal must be set upon the enemy's country." In other words, they had orders to destroy as many lives and as much virtue of women as they possibly could.

Successive German soldiers this brave and virtuous woman continued to resist. Finally, after a year and a half of fear and dread and continual struggle, the soldiers then in her home went to their officers and reported her as a quarrelsome, contentious woman, one who made a practise of insulting German soldiers. Those unspeakable cowards and brutes did this thing for revenge.

The authorities descended on the woman, took her children away from her by force, sent them to German institutions and sent her to work in a German-conquered mine in northern France. There the ultimate misery became hers. Her husband gone, her children torn from her, her home taken away, placed at degrading labor, her spirit broken, she fell a prey to German lust at last.

Only by yielding to the soldiers guarding the mine workers could she buy for herself the least privilege. Only by becoming worse than a slave could she obtain the slightest surcease from slavery.

She fell. For about a year she was tossed from one to another of the Huns in the neighborhood of that mine. Inevitably she became in time a menace to health, and then the Huns in Berlin ordered her deported. She was sent back through Switzerland to Evian with a card sewed to her rags, a card describing her as a syphilitic prostitute.

She was too crushed with suffering to make excuses for herself or to tell her story. There was nothing for the French government to do except send her to a hospital near Paris where such outcasts go to die. But Madame Doran did not die. She improved under treatment, and her distraught mind began to clear a little.

One day Madame Avril de Ste. Croix came to the hospital. Her angel pity and charity extends to the lowest outcasts among women, and she looks for possible curables among them everywhere. Attracted by the pure beauty of this victim, for she still retained some of her youthful loveliness, Madame de Ste. Croix spoke to her, and finally drew from her the terrible tale of her martyrdom.

At once Madame de Ste. Croix arranged for her removal to the house in Paris. There the best medical treatment, good nursing and kindness worked miracles. Madame Doran was soon on the road to partially restored life and health.

Meanwhile, Madame de Ste. Croix had sought and found the soldier husband. She told him what had befallen his wife and children. He heard with horror, then he dropped his head on the table before him and wept until his sleeves were drenched with tears. His bitterest grief spent, he raised his head and said:

"Madame, whatever my poor wife's condition, I can have no reproaches for her. I can remember only what she was to me in the past, a true, good wife. I loved her then and I love her now. Give her back to me, and for the rest of her life I will atone to her for what she has suffered."

This great-hearted French soldier had been wounded and was now mobilized in industry. He could make a home for his wife and Madame de Ste. Croix helped them establish themselves anew. Then she began a long search for the children. She wrote to the king of Spain, who is her friend and who, since the war began, has often used his influence with the German kaiser to find lost and imprisoned French and Belgians. The children of these poor parents were ultimately found and were restored to their bruised hearts.

Four of the five children were restored to them. The oldest boy, when the Germans broke up their home, resisted the soldiers sent to take them away. He was only a child. He did not realize the invincible majesty of Germany and he protested with all his young might. A German soldier kicked him, breaking his back. So he died, slowly and in great agony.

---

# CHAPTER XXII
# FRENCHMEN, NEVER FORGET

WITH Madame Avril de Ste. Croix I visited the house of mercy in Paris where women and child victims of German soldiers find refuge.

I visited this house and I saw there that which made me an implacable foe of any peace except on terms of extinction of the power that caused this war.

"We have very few here now," said Madame de Ste. Croix. "I mean compared with the first three years of the war. When the Germans think themselves victorious they are ruthless in their treatment of women and of civilians generally. When they are losing they are less cruel."

I am glad that I did not see the first fruits of German wrath. I do not understand how any one who did see it can ever smile or be happy again. What I have seen is the mild and tempered wrath of a beaten foe. I saw, in what is called the isolation pavilion of that house of mercy, seventeen girls in a condition of health which made it impossible for them to associate with others.

This pavilion had room for twice the number, and in former times, from 1914 to 1917, this one refuge was crowded, crowded with ruined and diseased French and Belgian girls. Now the German army has no time and less opportunity for such bestiality. There were only seventeen girls in the isolation pavilion of that house of mercy in Paris. The youngest girl was fourteen.

They have comfortable rooms, a little parlor with books and a piano, and a kind and devoted house mother. She is a teacher as well, and the education of these pathetic young creatures is carried on daily, as though they had a normal destiny, as indeed some of them have. Recovery, even from their dread malady, is not impossible, and the best medical care in Paris is given them freely.

In another pavilion of this house I saw another group of girls much better off. They had lived through horrors, but their health was somehow preserved. The youngest of these girls was twelve years old, and the hideous thing had happened to her two years ago. I think I have never seen a more tragic figure than this little girl. Her face was white and solemn and her eyes were old. She seldom spoke.

While we were looking at the sewing work and some of the girls were busy making us tea, a friend of the house came in to play the piano for the girls to sing. This is her regular contribution to the work. They sang, these poor little larks, standing around the piano, sang of home and love and all things beautiful.

I sat and listened and thought of peaceful America, where the war is still little more than an abstraction, a fact hardly realized except by the mothers and fathers and wives of men who have gone over.

Perhaps it was unworthy of a reporter, but the sight of these young French girls who have been forced, in the most ghastly fashion possible, to realize what this war means, was, for the moment, more than I could bear. I slipped away and ran to the farthest end of the enclosed garden.

Out of the sound of their voices I sat down and let the most unbearable part of the pain flow away in tears. As I sat there on that garden bench I heard a little soft exclamation. Looking up I saw the youngest girl, the little one who at ten years had had her life wrecked by a Hunnish criminal, more than one, for all I know. This child with the white solemn face and the old eyes stood there, pitying me for a trouble she did not understand. But for her there was only one trouble, and she assumed that I was weeping for that.

She reached out a timid little hand and laid it on mine.

"Ah, madame," she whispered, "is it not terrible, the war?"

It is terrible, but it has brought to the surface a heroism and a grandeur of soul that few of us knew the French people possessed. I asked Madame de Ste. Croix to tell me of the women and girls who had borne children to the German invaders. "What will you do with those boche babies?" I asked her.

"We shall assimilate them," she said proudly. And she added that the mothers, married or unmarried, as a rule loved their forlorn little babes. "I have known only two women who wished to get rid of their children," she assured me.

Nature is stronger than convention. The heart of woman is a mother heart, and nothing can ever change it. It was man and not woman who invented the myth of the illegitimate child.

Yet over there in France, even the men have risen above that harsh and cruel tradition. Madame de Ste. Croix, who takes on herself the painful duty of telling men what happened to their women when the Germans came, told me how nobly and bravely French men have stood by and sheltered them.

There was a girl who came under her care shortly before her baby was born. It was a fine little boy, fortunately the image of its mother. She had lost everything in the war, father, mother, home, and she clung passionately to her child. Only, at times, she wept bitterly thinking of the young soldier she had hoped to marry, and who was ignorant of what had befallen her.

Madame de Ste. Croix looked up the young man, found his regiment, and arranged a meeting with him. His agony when she told him was great, but not for an instant was his allegiance to his sweetheart shaken. He had mourned her as dead and he blessed the noble woman who restored her to him again.

"What has happened is not conceivably her fault," declared this fine young soldier. "I love her more for what she has suffered. If I could I would marry her to-morrow and be a father to her child. But I am not sure that I can. I am not sure that it would be for her happiness."

With tears in his eyes the man told Madame de Ste. Croix that he was under twenty-five, and until after a man has passed that age he may not, according to French law, marry without the consent of his mother. This young man's parents, he explained, were small town folk with a small town point of view.

Their morality was a little narrow-minded, and he feared that they would never consent to his marriage with a girl who had suffered at the hands of the Hun. They would pity her, of course, but they would not want her for a daughter. They would never be able to love the child.

"Let me go away now," he implored, "and try to think what is best to be done."

A week later he returned with a radiant face. He had obtained leave and had gone home to see his mother. There, on his knees, he had told her a lie, one that must have been recorded in Heaven to his favor. He told her that he was the father of that girl's baby, that he had wronged her, and now begged permission to right the wrong by marrying her.

The mother's reproaches were severe, and the poor young man had the pain of seeing her suffer for what she thought was his guilt. But after she had been induced to look at the baby's picture her good heart was · awakened. She agreed to the marriage and promised to love and care for the mother and child until the end of the war.

This man was a simple soldier, a child of working people. He did not know that he was heroic, and in fact what he did has been matched by scores of men in France. Very often after the Germans violated women and children in the invaded towns and villages, they murdered them cruelly. Those left alive have been cherished by their men, only too thankful that they were spared.

"Not that the men do not suffer," said Madame de Ste. Croix. "We prize virtue and stainlessness in women. But we love justice more. And if this dreadful thing is hard on men whose betrothed are wronged, how much harder it is on a man whose wife has borne children to the brutal boche.

"He may forget what she has gone through, but how can he endure the presence of the child? What will be the future of those children, intruders in the family? I do not know."

What has happened to thousands of women and girls in invaded Belgium and France could just as well happen in this country. It would happen without the smallest doubt if the Huns landed on our shores. Can you picture it? Can you imagine what it would be, fathers and mothers of America, to stand with German guns leveled at your heads while beasts in human form violated your young daughters before your eyes?

Can you imagine what it would be for our soldiers to come home from the war and find their wives and daughters with German babies in their arms? This is what many French and Belgian soldiers have had to endure. You will not persuade any of these men to listen to arguments in favor of a peace without victory.

All over France you will see in homes, in shop windows, on blank walls a poster. There are just three words on this poster: "Frenchmen, never forget!" In the upper right-hand corner of the poster there is a picture of some woeful thing that has happened since the German hordes began to overrun the world.

Sometimes the picture is of a burned and desolated village, a shattered hulk of what was once a beautiful old church. Oftener it is a picture of ruined womanhood, blasted childhood.

In the lower left-hand corner of the poster is a picture of a smooth German salesman trying to sell something in France. "Frenchmen, never forget!" They never will forget. They have tenacious memories, our French allies.

Can any one who has visited Paris forget the statue of Strasbourg in the Place de la Concorde? It is one of eight splendid monuments in that square, each representing a city of France. When the Germans filched Alsace and Lorraine from France, after the war of 1870, Strasbourg was lost to the French. On that day they laid funeral wreaths on the statue in the Place de la Concorde, and they have kept funeral wreaths there ever since.

Until August, 1914. Then they took away the emblem of mourning, because they knew Strasbourg would be theirs again. The statue is gay with flowers now, and with flags of all the allies. Our flag is there, the flag the French call *le drapeau étoilé*, the bestarred banner. May it stay there until what it has gone to France for has been accomplished, until the utterly crushed and vanquished German army has been pursued beyond the Rhine, until something of what the women of France and of martyred Belgium have endured has been paid for.

Not in the same coin, however. The men who have suffered so bravely are incapable of such crimes.

---

# CHAPTER XXIII
# THE NEW WOMAN IN FRANCE

THE long-distance gun which has been bombarding Paris has not terrorized the civil population, as the Germans intended. I was in and out of the city for a month after the gun began to do its deadly work, and I can attest to that fact. But I remember three occasions when the wrath of the Parisians rose to such a height that I shuddered to think of the retribution that was piling up for Germany.

The first time was when a shell struck an historic old church, killing seventy-five Good Friday worshipers. The second was when the shell burst in a ward of a maternity hospital, making victims of mothers and newly born babes. The third time was when a factory was struck, and at least seven women workers were savagely slain. The shell struck the front of the factory, killing the head foreman who was just leaving the place. The man was torn limb from limb.

The entire front wall of the factory crushed inward and fell upon the women seated at their work. Six were killed outright, one died on the way to the hospital, and thirty were desperately hurt. They were nearly all war widows, wives of soldiers and refugees, those slain women and their comrades in the factory.

"After the church, after the nursery, the sewing room," wrote the editor of *Le Matin.* "It will be said that the barbarians respect nothing." Not religion, not infancy, not womanhood.

What deepened the indignation in the minds of the French public was the almost sublime courage shown by the women in that factory. There was not a single moment of panic. Instantly picking themselves up, those who were unhurt began to lift out of the mass of bricks and shattered timbers the dead and wounded. They vied with one another in their calm, quick efforts to save life, and by the time the ambulances arrived all the wounded had received first aid. The next morning at the usual hour every woman, except the seriously wounded, reported for work. Not one stayed at home.

"France can not spare workers now," said one woman to President Poincaré, who personally visited the wrecked factory to congratulate these heroines.

Such is the metal of French wives and mothers, who have always, until this war, lived rather secluded lives within their own homes. In sheer admiration the French men, who have hitherto monopolized the higher fields of industry, and who have laughed at the idea of women in political life, are now ready to yield to any demands that women may in future put forth.

French women can probably have the vote for the asking. They have not made up their minds, in great numbers, that they want to vote. But the suffrage movement is well started, it has good leaders, women of education and social power, and there is no question as to the outcome.

War has wrought great changes in the status of women in all the countries directly involved, and in France it has almost overturned the whole social theory. The rigid system of chaperonage of girls has been greatly relaxed.

For this the Red Cross has been responsible to a certain degree. Thousands of young women who never in their lives before saw a man except in the presence of their mothers now work in station canteens at all hours of the day and night, cooking, serving, feeding soldiers and refugees, waiting on the sick and weary with tireless devotion.

I have spoken of the dearth of conductors on the French trains. There is one train attendant who never fails, and that is the young woman who collects funds for the Red Cross. Every time a train stops it is boarded by girls and women in white uniforms, who go through all the carriages shaking tin money receptacles. These are about the size and shape of a quart milk bottle, and the girl who holds it neglects nobody. "*Pour la Croix Rouge! Pour les blessés!*" she cries, and everybody drops small change into the milk bottle's insatiable maw. In the course of a long journey one contributes rather heavily. But then, one should.

The educated women of France have gone in for hospital nursing as never before. No part of unpreparedness in France was more serious than the neglect of the nursing profession. Formerly almost all nursing was done by the religious orders, and to tell the truth, it was not very scientific nursing. If a sister happened to be a born nurse, so much the better. But even the best of them were untrained in the modern sense.

When the religious orders were broken up in France little or nothing was publicly done to replace the nurses. I visited a house in Paris, a sort of a nurses' settlement, where for some years a highly educated and philanthropic woman has maintained a small training school of her own.

This woman, whose name, unfortunately, has slipped my memory, lives and works in a crowded quarter of the city where there is much tuberculosis. She established her nurses' training school in connection with her tuberculosis work, which is extensive. She induced a number of educated girls to take up nursing, and many of them in 1914 went into war work. But they were a drop in the bucket. They were dozens where thousands were needed. So the women had to leave their homes, as our leisured women will have to, if this war outlasts 1918, and made themselves capable and devoted trained nurses.

These are the new women of France, and it would be extraordinary if, after finding freedom from the old restrictions and conventions, they should ever go back to the old ways. I met several women who were as emancipated as any young American feminist, and who seemed very happy in their new independence.

At Aix-les-Bains, where our soldiers went for their first vacation leaves, there was a young girl who was an almost startling example. She was about twenty years old and very pretty, in a delicate, patrician way. Before the war this girl would never have gone out of the house unattended. She had been educated in a private school with girls of her own social class, and but for the war would have been married by this time to a man chosen for her in the family council.

Now she was driving her own little Ford ambulance for the benefit of the American soldiers. She had joined the American Y. M. C. A., wore its becoming gray and blue uniform, with a boy's soft hat pulled down over her bobbed black hair, and she was as busy as a maternal little wren.

I don't know where she and the little car had operated before, but when the boys began to arrive at Aix she drove down from Paris, entirely alone except for a girl chum, an English girl, I believe, and a dozen times a day she sat at the wheel speeding between Aix and Chambéry, four miles away, carting supplies from one Y. M. C. A. headquarters to the other, and taking soldiers back and forth as well.

Mademoiselle Marcelle spoke English quaintly but fluently, but she was not a very conversational young person. She was grave and very dignified, and she loved all American soldiers too well to favor any one very much. They treated her like a princess and were ready any minute to clean the car, or oil it, or spend half a day doing things to its insides.

She was a charming little creature, Mademoiselle Marcelle. My son confided in me one evening that he didn't think he would have to look farther for his life's ideal, but then, so did at least a dozen other doughboys, so I considered his chances rather slim.

Even before the war the position of the French girl showed signs of change. The quality of her education had immensely improved, and in fact was practically the same as that of boys. Coeducation was unknown in the schools and in higher institutions, but in the Sorbonne, the oldest of all French universities, men and women attended the same lectures.

There have been individual parents who desired the fullest freedom for their daughters, and who educated them for the professions. There are not many women doctors in France, but the woman lawyer is highly respected and even encouraged.

One daughter of such modern parents is at present rendering good service to her country in the French foreign office. Mademoiselle St. René Taillandier is a member of the press section of the foreign office, and because of her fluent English is of the greatest assistance to English and American correspondents, especially women correspondents.

Mademoiselle St. René Taillandier's father is a veteran member of the diplomatic corps, and her mother is a very modern minded woman. Having lived in many countries of the world, and observing the constantly widening field of women's activities, they agreed that their daughter should be brought up as an English or an American girl. She was given a sound education, part of it in England, and she was allowed the fullest possible freedom of choice and action.

Very recently having received at the Sorbonne a degree corresponding to our master of arts, this fortunate young French woman has entered upon a most promising literary career. She has acted in the capacity of secretary to the famous novelist, Paul Bourget, and it was he who discovered her literary gift and insisted upon her developing it. Her first stories were published in the dignified *Revue des Deux Mondes*, and have just appeared in book form.

These changes in the status of women are going to be very good for France and her people. Already one sees their broadening effect. In the old days the French showed a certain lack of hospitality to strangers. You had to be very well known to a French family before you were invited to visit the house. This is the real reason why the French have been so little understood.

It has been said of them that they had no word for home, hence they must be less domestic than other people. They have a word for home. It is "*foyer*," which means literally hearth. The family hearth was to them so sacred that they couldn't bring themselves to admit foreigners there.

That, too, is changing. Not only middle class people, but people of wealth are opening their homes, especially to Americans. I received the most unexpected invitations to the homes of almost strangers. One woman of prominence whom I met for the first time told me that she had a country house in Brittany which she wanted to place at the disposal of American soldiers this summer.

"I have lost several near relatives in the war," she said, "and it would be a consolation to me to feel that I was doing something for the ally that came in time to save our France from perishing. I want to know the American young man. If your son should be so unfortunate as to be wounded I hope I can take him to my house for his convalescence. I would gladly receive him and any of the American soldiers."

The kaiser's atrocious war, meant to crush and alienate and enslave the English, French and Americans, has had quite another effect. It has brought us into new and noble friendship. It has forged ties that never will be broken.

# CHAPTER XXIV
# POUR LA PATRIE

IN one of the most widely read of French magazines I came across a story which illustrates the wonderful spirit and loyalty of the French mother. She loves her children with a devotion unsurpassed anywhere. But more deeply and more deathlessly she loves France.

The story was contained in an article written by a French correspondent who witnessed the repatriation at Evian-les-Bains of a large number of women and children long held prisoners by the Germans. Among them was a woman and her two little boys, Jean, aged five, and Gilbert, three. The mother was in the last stages of tuberculosis, and she had just managed to live long enough to get her children to Evian. Then she died. But before she died she said to the French Red Cross representative who had promised to care for the little ones: "I want you to make workmen of them. The country will so much need skilled workers."

This heroic mother, who with her last breath dedicated her children to the rebuilding of France, was a simple, plain woman of the people. It is hardly likely that she had ever said a single word about patriotism. She lived it, and so do all French women. And there, I verily believe, is the secret of the vitality and the unconquerable strength of the French nation. At their mother's knee the men of France learn that the first love and allegiance of their hearts and lives are due their country. They never forget that lesson.

I do not know who ever invented the fiction that French women are not maternal. It is true that they do not, as a rule, have many children, but that is easily understood when one studies the French economic and social conditions. In all families outside the wage earning class the girl children must be provided with dowries. It is the custom, and a dowerless girl has a difficult time getting married. Also, under French law, all children inherit equally their parents' estate. Land holdings, as a rule, are very moderate, and if there were many children it would be impossible to educate and equip them for life.

It has never been the custom, as with us, for girls of the middle classes to earn their living. Until very recently the *jeune fille*, the young, unmarried girl, hardly ever went out unescorted. The prototype of our American college bred, tennis playing, independent, self-supporting girl did not exist in France. The one ideal of the gently reared French girl was marriage and a home. And in the home she became a real power.

Theoretically all women are powers in their homes. The power of the French wife and mother is not theoretical, it is real, it is legalized. A Frenchman who does not consult his wife in every business matter is the exception. A son who does not refer all his affairs to his mother's consideration is a bad son. Under French law the family council, which includes near relatives as well as fathers and mothers, settles most questions involving minor children. It is in the family council where marriages are arranged and marriage contracts agreed upon.

Women rule these family councils to a very great extent. Their voices in all domestic matters are listened to with respect. You will see bearded men give up a cherished project, even a love match, because *Maman* could not be persuaded of its wisdom. A man can not legally marry without his mother's consent until he is twenty-five years old.

Because of their great power in the home French women have not left the domestic life to the same extent that English and American women have done. They have not insisted on entering all the trades and professions. They have not demanded the vote. But the war has brought great changes into French life, and the women of France will never again be as they were before. They, too, must go out and work. They must accept the responsibilities of political life. They must socialize their maternal love. They are doing it already.

When the Germans invaded northern France in 1914, when most of the men were swept away into the fighting, the women assumed the burden not only of family life but of community life as well. Often the German commander, entering a town or village and demanding the presence of the mayor, would be met by a stout, gray-haired matron who would calmly announce, "I am the mayor."

So she was, and had been since *monsieur le maire* had been mobilized, or perhaps murdered by the invading Huns. Many a French town and village with its hapless population has been saved from utter annihilation by the intrepid courage and determination of a woman in authority. More than once the woman was a nun.

France knows better than ever of what stuff its women are made, and the future status of the women is absolutely theirs to decide. There is plenty of evidence that they will decide on more independence and a wider range of activities.

I visited French munitions works, including the famous Citroen factory in Paris, where shells for France's celebrated 75's are turned out. I sat down at luncheon in the vast canteen of the factory with thousands of workers, fully half of them women. Before the war most of those women would have been engaged in sewing work at home, at very low wages. Seclusion of women went with family self-respect.

Now the girls were working in a shell factory. They were in overalls, some of them, and they were doing men's work. All through this tremendous establishment I met girls driving motor shell carriers at high speed. I saw them working in the flaming forge rooms. I saw them cutting through steel bars with acetylene torches. I saw them at lathes shaping shells. I saw them making bullets. They work ten hours a day, where eight had been the legal limit before the war. They do not complain. It is for France, *pour la patrie.*

There has not been, as there was in England, a great pouring into industry of the women of the middle classes. The women workers were recruited from the home workers and from the luxury trades, so-called. There were many more of these in France, which was the finery mine for all the world, than in other countries. Thousands of girls and women who made clothes and hats and *bijoux* were thrown out of work and were easily transferred to the munitions trades.

They seem to like the change. They are a much more coquettish class than the English workers. They do not wear any hats, as a rule, but they spend a good part of their wages on their hair. Even in the factory a girl in overalls working at a forge has her black hair elaborately coiffured and shining with brilliantine. Usually her hair is dressed with bright pins and sidecombs. What the French working girls would do if the war lasts long enough to exhaust the world's supply of rhinestone combs I really do not know.

The French woman who escorted me through the Citroen factory deplored the fact that the working girls are beginning to wear dressy clothes and high heeled boots. It did not used to be so, she said. I pointed out that the girls formerly hadn't the money to buy these things, and that the evils of democracy were cured only by more democracy. Women can't learn, all at once, how to spend wisely.

The women of the French middle classes and those of the old aristocracy have gone into war work, if not into war industries. The advent of so many more women in factory work brought a new sense of responsibility to the more fortunately placed women. They have done a great deal for the workers to keep them in health and strength, to take care of the children of married workers, and even to raise wages.

The Citroen factory is such a model establishment that it has been written about in half a dozen American papers and magazines. It pays very good wages, and the minimum for piece work, eight francs a day—about a dollar and forty-five cents—is shared by men and women alike. Most of the workers average ten and twelve francs a day.

In this factory an excellent noon meal is served at cost, about thirty cents, with wine extra. The meal is prepared by professional cooks in spotless kitchens and it is well served. But not every factory has a canteen, and many have been established and are maintained by women of wealth for the benefit of the workers. I visited one of these in company with the principal founder, formerly a woman of the exclusive "great world," but now a hard and indefatigable worker.

"These girls must have good food," she said. "It is a tradition in France, and if we lose it we lose something national. We who have time must feed those who have no time except for toil."

The luncheon served at this canteen was as dainty, and it was perhaps even more carefully composed, than an expensive repast in a Fifth avenue tea room. The rich lady and her American guest sat down and ate it with the girls from the munitions factory a block away, and we enjoyed it as much as they did.

Every American woman knows the beautifully embroidered French underwear, which over here is rather expensive but in France could once be purchased for very little. The Paris "white sales" before the war was the trade event of the year for women. But what few women took into consideration when buying this lovely underwear so cheaply was that the women who made the garments received appallingly low wages for their work.

The underwear was made by women working at home. Pride kept them from leaving home, and besides, there were often young children to care for. So the home workers toiled far into the night, sewing and embroidering the dainty things that were to adorn the soft bodies of richer women. For their long toil they often received less than a franc a day.

I met the woman who was chiefly responsible for the alleviation of this great blot on the civilization of France. Her name is Madame Viollet, and she has devoted her life to the problems of the poor, in much the same wholehearted way as Jane Addams, Julia Lathrop, Lillian Wald and other well-known American women have. Like them she lives with her poor.

The problem of the home worker was long her chief province, and since the war she has succeeded in having a minimum wage law passed through the French Chamber of Deputies and the Senate, giving to the women who work at home four or five times as much as they ever received before.

"I do not wish all women to work in factories," she said to me. "Expectant mothers, women with young children, delicate women, ought to stay at home. And, since they must earn, it is the business of the state to see that they are not cheated."

Not only did Madame Viollet secure for the home workers a minimum wage, she organized them into a *syndicat*, or union, to enforce the law, and to raise their own status in various ways. This was a remarkable thing to do, because French women are totally unused to the idea of trade unions. The men rarely admit them to their unions, and the strong woman labor leader of England and the United States is practically unknown. But the home workers are organized now, and after the war we shall pay more for our French embroidered underwear.

# CHAPTER XXV
## BY WAY OF DIVERSION

I SHALL never hear that musical classic, *Where Do We Go From Here?*, without remembering a young lieutenant I tried to be a mother to in France. I really led the young man terribly astray, and but for a bit of luck at the end I might have got him court-martialed.

The whole thing grew out of the fact that so many of the men in France are mobilized that they haven't enough left for train conductors and station guards. You can travel for hundreds of miles in France and never have your ticket taken up by anybody. I have a collection of French railroad tickets which I bought and used, but never had to show to a conductor.

One of these tickets entitled me to ride first class from Bourges to a certain large American military camp. I bought the ticket one morning last spring and was informed by the polite Frenchman behind the wicket that it would be necessary for me to change at a junction about midway in the journey.

"They allow you barely five minutes to make the change," he warned me, "but you can not miss the train. It is the Paris express."

We were slightly delayed, and when I reached the junction I made a quick leap to the station platform and looked around for my train. There were several standing there, so I ran, suit-case in one hand and typewriter in the other, in search of a guard. There was only one, but I hailed him and asked him to indicate the Paris express.

"Platform three," he exclaimed. "But, hurry, hurry, madame. Already the train he marches." And surely enough the queer little tin whistle which is a characteristic of French trains was shrilling its starting signal and the doors of the carriages were slamming.

I dashed across the tracks and almost into a young officer who was looking wildly around and calling in English for a porter. Seeing my O. D. uniform, he recognized a compatriot, and implored me to tell him, if I knew, which train he should take to go to Y———.

"Come along," I flung back at him, for I was still racing for that moving train. "I'm going there, too."

We just made it, flinging my suit-case and typewriter in, and falling in after them ourselves. The lieutenant had no luggage.

I was tired, having been up late the night before, and without any more conversation I curled up in a corner and went to sleep. I must have slept for an hour, and after I awoke the train rolled on for another hour without coming to Y——.

We were alone in the compartment, and no conductor appeared. So I spoke to the young officer. "I thought Y—— was only about an hour and a half from the junction," I remarked.

"I thought so, too," he answered. "But I don't speak a word of French, so I don't always get very precise information."

"Well, the guard told me that this was the Paris express," I said. "We must be on the right train."

We commented on the singular lack of train conductors, and the lieutenant said yes, you could travel all over France free if you had luck. He had traveled for forty-eight hours for one franc and eighty centimes. At least, the only ticket he had been asked to surrender cost one franc eighty. The rest were in his pocket.

But he didn't enjoy traveling alone in a foreign country. He couldn't even ask for a match in French, much less inquire about trains. I resolved that I would be nice to that young man and see that he got safely to his destination. But when another hour went by and we still didn't reach Y—— it occurred to me that I might not be very much of a guide. I opened my suit-case, got out a map of France, found the junction from which we had started and watched for the name on the next station.

We were on the Paris express all right, but we were going to Paris instead of away from it, as I had intended. We were within a mile or two from the city of Orleans. I broke the news to the lieutenant and he turned a little pale. He simply had to get to Y—— that night, he said. He was on a special mission and had been charged to deliver his message as quickly as possible.

"Even if we get there this evening," he added, "I don't know how I am going to get out to the camp. They don't allow officers to sleep in the town, you know. They know I'm on the way because I sent all my luggage on ahead."

"Perhaps there is a train back very soon," I suggested. "We'll get off at Orleans and I will inquire."

We did, the lieutenant carrying my suit-case, and both of us hurrying as fast as we could to the ticket office. What was the next train for Y——? The next train was about to start. "Hurry, hurry, madame and monsieur. You will miss it unless you run. It is necessary to change at X," mentioning the very junction where our unfortunate lives had been joined.

We ran, without stopping to buy tickets, and scrambled breathlessly aboard the moving train. Nobody asked us for any tickets, and we actually traveled the entire distance back to X without paying the French government a single *sou*. We arrived about seven o'clock, dusk, with our final destination still forty-five miles ahead. Moreover, there was no train before midnight.

The young lieutenant was very blue, but he agreed that there was no use worrying, and we might as well go up-town and get some dinner. We would have to go together, whether we liked it or not, because he couldn't get along alone. We had a good dinner, and by the time it was finished it selfishly occurred to me that I had had about enough of that strange young man's society. It was obvious that he had had enough of mine, because it is a little bit dangerous for an American officer to be seen in a lady's company in France. Officers are not supposed to have women friends or relatives on that side of the ocean, and if a member of the military police were to see him carrying a woman's suit-case through a civilian town the policeman soldier might develop a little curiosity. And what a fishy story we had to tell after all. Childish!

"I think," said I to the lieutenant, "that you can get along all right now. I am very tired and I believe I will take a room in this hotel and stay over until to-morrow."

He brightened up amazingly and said that it was a capital idea. But when I asked for a room the little *patronne* declared that she didn't have a bed in the house. Perhaps I could get one at the hotel opposite the station. I couldn't, nor did I find a room vacant in any one of the other hotels.

"Well," I said, "I'm not going to get into Y—— after midnight. It's a small place, and I am not sure I can get a room there. I'm going back to Bourges. There are large hotels there, and there's a train at ten."

"I can't get to Y—— after midnight either," gloomed the lieutenant. "There won't be any place for me to stay, and at that hour I couldn't telephone the camp to send an ambulance for me. I'll have to go to Bourges, too."

To Bourges we went, and in addition to getting a room for myself I had to take the lieutenant along and get a room for him. Why had I ever met the man? Why had he ever met me? Would we never get rid of each other, or were we tied for life?

The next day we met at an early luncheon and again we set out for X. "Remember," I warned him, "we shall have barely time at the junction to make that other train. I know which track it is on now. We'll all be ready to jump when this one stops."

But our train was shunted on to a side track a little way out of Bourges, in order to let some troop trains pass. We were late, and we got into X just in time to see the train for Y—— disappear around a curve.

"See here," I said to the pale and despairing man, "I do not propose to spend the rest of my life traveling between this wretched junction and the city of Bourges. I have already spent twenty-four hours traveling thirty-five miles. At this rate I might die of old age before I got back to America. You go up-town and find a motor-car, anything that will go, and we'll finish the journey in that."

"How can I expect to find a motor-car?" cried the lieutenant. "You know as well as I do that no pleasure automobiles are allowed to run in France, and this hole won't have any taxi-cabs. Besides a taxi down to Y—— would set us back two or three hundred francs."

"Never you mind about that," I retorted. "You do what you are told. You go straight up-town and look for a car."

We quarreled by this time, like a real married pair, and with quite the air of a defeated husband he departed on his quest. In a short time he came back. Of course, there was no motor-car to be had, he reported, but he had had some luck. A colonel's limousine had broken down somewhere in the neighborhood and it was being towed down to Y—— by an army truck. He had heavily subsidized the doughboys who were accompanying the truck, and they had agreed to stop on a certain corner long enough for us to surreptitiously get into the limousine.

It was a beautiful car, apparently in pre-war days the property of some woman of fashion. The upholstery was pale French gray and there were all sorts of scent bottles, tablets and flower holders in silver and cut glass. But it was a terribly open limousine, all windows, and the lieutenant and I were conspicuous objects. The old truck that towed us made a lot of noise, and at every village we passed through the people ran to the doors and windows and cheered vociferously with delighted laughter.

The worst was getting into the camp at Y——, but here the bit of luck appeared. It began to rain just before we arrived, and when we rolled in the rain was coming down in such sheets that everybody except the men on guard were under cover. Nobody saw us but the soldiers who examined our passes. So the lieutenant's military career was saved.

We never met again. The lieutenant, I am sure, hopes we never shall.

# CHAPTER XXVI
# WHEN THE BOYS COME HOME

SHOULD you happen to be in Paris or in any other French city in the early spring, you will witness an amusing and at the same time an inspiring sight; the carnival of the military class of the year before going into training camps.

France has lived next door to a burglar nation for nearly half a century. Ever since Alsace-Lorraine was stolen from her in 1871, France has known this, and she has therefore retained the system of compulsory military service.

Every year, on the eighteenth of April, all able-bodied young Frenchmen who have reached the age of twenty go up for a two years' military training. Just before the war the term was lengthened to three years. Their term completed, they are placed in the reserves, ready at any time to be mobilized and fight.

The world well remembers how in late July, 1914, the tocsin sounded all over France, calling from field and factory, counting room and office the glorious citizen army that rushed out against the barbarian invasion, turned it at the Marne, and saved the life of civilization.

I believe that after this war some form of compulsory military service will be enacted in this country. Let us rather call it required military service, since in a democracy such service is agreed upon as a wise policy and is not forced on the people without their consent. The American form might well be something like that of France.

Proof that military service there is not in the least oppressive is the gaiety with which the young cadets greet their term of training. It has long been the custom for the year's class to make a carnival of its going. Beginning two or three weeks before the date set for their encampment, groups of these lads, fantastically arrayed and decorated, would parade through the streets, singing their favorite choruses, making a great deal of noise between songs, shouting and chaffing the passers-by.

No youth considered himself properly dressed without a huge *boutonnière*, sometimes of flowers but oftener a paper monstrosity as big as a cabbage. Sometimes a lad appeared with a buttonhole bouquet of vegetables. Anything for a joke. Thus dressed, furnished with a guitar or an accordion, "the bunch," as our slang would call them, fared forth to have a last good time before going under discipline. For the time being they owned the town, and nobody complained of their noise or their pranks.

I had seen this before the war, but I was unprepared to see the custom retained. Yet this April in Paris, in Bordeaux, and several other cities I saw the same singing groups, the same absurd decorations, the same fun-making. The class of 1918 was younger than the class of 1914, but it was every bit as exuberant. Four years of war and desolation, of sickening anxiety and cruel bereavement, were powerless to depress the spirit of young France.

Early on the morning of April eighteenth I started on a journey from the Orleans station, and there, filling the place with laughter and excited conversation, I saw about a hundred of the class of 1918 leave for their cantonment.

Their mothers and fathers and sweethearts were there seeing them off, just as we have been seeing our boys off to training camps this year. But these French fathers and mothers have suffered bitter losses. Hardly a family in France that has not known bereavement. Most of the women I saw that April morning wore deep mourning.

Even though they wept in their hearts, they sent their boys away with laughter and brave cheer. With bantering words on their lips, their hearts were saying: "O France, loved Mother, take one more of my sons. Like those who have died he was mine only until you needed him more."

Their train left the station ahead of mine, and until it was far down the line these great fathers and mothers continued to wave and cheer. Then they clasped hands and silently went home.

After four years of war. It made me ashamed of every wavering moment I have allowed myself since we entered this conflict.

This is a time when the women of America must take stock of themselves, when they must consider whether or not they have grown up to the stature of the women overseas; whether they can keep step with the men who have gone over to fight beside the French, English, Belgian and Italian soldiers. For those women of the world war are very great in mind and spirit. Those young Americans are growing fast. They will never be the same again.

We sing about keeping the home fires burning, "Till the boys come home." But we have got to face one big fact. When the boys come home they will have become men, and men of a totally different type than any to which we have been accustomed. They will be bigger, broader, finer, in body and mind. They will be better educated. They will expect more of their women.

In the first place our men, when they come home, will be such perfect physical specimens that they will be astonished to see women who are flat chested, or fat, sallow skinned or heavy-eyed. They won't have much patience with indigestion and headaches. That kind of thing goes with slacking over there.

There ought to be a great big, earnest health movement among women in this country during the rest of the war. We see signs of it in the farmerettes, the campers, the women police.

The men in France are learning new things every day. They have traveled. They have had a chance to compare their country with others, their compatriots with other people.

We have been called a nation of boasters. We boasted of our achievements because most of us never had a chance to see anything of the achievements of other nations. These men have.

They know now that French cities are often far more beautiful than American cities. If they lack skyscrapers they have ancient castles and châteaux. What the French build they build beautifully and for the ages.

You never hear any boasting from Americans in France. Our men are learning humility. They know that we do some things well, but they know that we have much to learn from the older civilizations, and they are out to learn.

A young engineer over there told me how when the Americans began to double track the French railways and to build the miles on miles of switches necessary to handle trainloads of supplies for the armies, the French were shocked at the shoddy work done.

"You know how it is with us," he said. "When we are doing a hurry job in laying rails we drive spikes in every other tie. The French drive them twice in every tie, and they rivet them after they are driven through. We do that now, over here. The French won't stand for anything else. They say they won't risk railroad accidents for their troops."

Our men are getting a wonderful education, not only through their army experience and their faculties of observation, but through the Y. M. C. A. department of lectures and entertainment. At first the idea was simply to entertain the men in their leisure hours, to furnish music and moving pictures and vaudeville. But the men themselves soon called for better things, and the Y. M. C. A. is preparing to give what amounts almost to university extension courses in the camps. Books in unlimited quantities are being shipped overseas by the American Public Library Association. Text-books, reference books for every branch of study.

This spring Anson Phelps Stokes, secretary of Yale University, went to France, and was made head of the committee on education in the Y. M. C. A. in the field. Mr. Stokes made a thorough canvass of the situation, visiting many camps, consulting with army authorities and with the men themselves. He visited the camps and canteens of the English Y. M. C. A. in order to compare their work with ours.

The programme of education was not complete when I left, but I saw a tentative plan which by this time must have been worked into something truly admirable. The men of our army are going to be given a real practical education. Those behind the lines who wish to continue a college or technical course, dropped when the draft law went into effect, will be able to do so. Those whose early education was neglected will have a chance to go back to elementary school.

Men who do not care to take up any serious studies will hear lectures, if they choose, in which they will learn a great deal about French and English history. In the very region, perhaps the very town, where great events of history took place, they will hear the story told. The past will become real. It will help our men to understand the present.

I know that our soldiers are thirsty for this kind of an education. I was asked by the Y. M. C. A. to lecture in some of the camps on what I saw of the Russian revolution. It was with great reluctance that I agreed to try one lecture. It did not seem possible to me that soldiers, tired with the day's labor, would care to listen to such a subject.

"I will try it once or even twice, if you like," I told the secretary, "but I'm afraid it won't get across."

It did. I spoke something like thirty times, and every time to crowded rooms. I spoke in sheds, tents, theaters, town halls, and even in the open. I never had such audiences. Their eyes were keen and bright and they drank in every word. Afterward they crowded around asking questions.

These men are not going to be interested in women who never read anything but novels and the cheap magazines, who know nothing about geography or history or politics. They will want to talk over their experiences with their mothers and sisters and wives, and if they can not listen intelligently the men are going to be disappointed.

Hundreds of soldiers with whom I talked showed me pictures of their women at home. They said loving things, proud things, but the women they were proudest of were those who were doing some kind of real war service. "My sister Elizabeth is the head of the Red Cross canteen at the union station in my town. They feed hundreds of men every time a troop train goes through."

"My wife is pretty busy these days, with the children and her surgical dressings classes."

These are the things the men like to think of their women doing while they are away. They see the women workers in the canteens of the Red Cross and the Y. M. C. A. in France. They see nurses and women ambulance drivers working regardless of weariness, careless of danger. They see all around them unselfish, courageous service. The spirit is in the air over there, and the men like to feel that their women at home are like that, too.

When the boys come home they want to come back to women who have been born again into high and noble patriotism. "Not only hats off to the flag. Sleeves up for the flag." That slogan, adopted by the men in the steel industries who are speeding up the building of ships, ships, and more ships, is the patriotism our men are living every day in France, and it is the kind they have a right to expect of the women at home.

# CHAPTER XXVII
## WHAT KIND OF WAR WORK

MRS. ROTHSCHILD, of Kensington Palace Green, a street in an exclusive residence district of West London, is president of a society for the distribution of Jewish literature among English Jews serving at the front, or wounded in hospitals. Not long ago the society held a large mass meeting in a seaside resort where many wealthy Jewish people go in summer.

The object of the meeting was to raise money, and Mrs. Rothschild made a special journey from her country home, a distance of twenty or thirty miles, to the resort. She did this in her zeal to make her pet war work a success, but—in so doing she broke a law of Great Britain, got herself arrested and was fined sixty shillings, about fourteen dollars and fifty cents.

For Mrs. Rothschild, ignoring the fact that gasoline is so scarce in England that most pleasure motor-cars have been retired and automobiling, except for war purposes, has been practically eliminated, deliberately hired a car to take her from her home to the meeting.

The zealous Mrs. Rothschild knew the law. She could not help knowing it, because every private car in Great Britain and almost all taxi-cabs have huge gas bags on top, and are driven by gas instead of petrol, as they call it there. But all she thought of was her war work and her mass meeting.

There are not many such women in Great Britain, but every once in a while they are caught and fined. Marie Corelli, the novelist, an ardent patriot on the surface, was heavily fined for food hoarding. At a time when food was terribly scarce in England, when even the rich went without meat, butter or sugar, and many working people ate dry bread and canned salmon, Miss Corelli's secret larder was found to be stocked with hams, bacon, butter, sugar, tea, and all manner of delicacies to last for nearly a year.

I remember another woman of prominence who had seventeen Persian cats for whom she managed somehow to buy cream. When she was arraigned she pleaded in extenuation that the cats were used to cream, and that she gave three days every week to canteen work at one of the railroad stations. The flinty-hearted judge fined her nevertheless and threatened her with a prison sentence unless the cats' diet was placed on a war footing.

These instances are mentioned in order to illustrate a condition of things to which we here in the United States are not altogether strangers. I was in Europe ten months out of the first year of our participation in the war, and when I returned in May I was naturally delighted to find signs that the country was thoroughly awakened, and to learn that almost every woman I knew was up to her eyes in war work.

I knew already that American women generally were aiding food conservation, saving meat, wheat and sugar for the allies, for what the United States has voluntarily sacrificed to feed Europe has done more to earn the friendship and gratitude of our allies than anything else we could have done. It is placed on a par with our war loans of money. It has redeemed us from the reputation of being dollar worshipers.

There is no question of our zeal and our generosity. There may be a question of our efficiency as war workers. It is not enough to conserve food. We must conserve effort as well. There is no reason why we should repeat the mistakes made by our allies in the beginning of the war. Just as we are benefiting from their experience in fighting Germans in the trenches, we should take advantage of their experience in war service behind the lines.

Their experience has convinced them that it is better to have a few large organizations at work than to have many small ones. It is better for various reasons. One reason is that every community has people like Mrs. Rothschild and the lady with the seventeen Persian cats. They give with one hand and waste with the other.

Another reason why it is better to support the Red Cross and the Y. M. C. A. than, for example, to form a society for furnishing enlisted men with special comforts, is that many such societies mean a duplication of effort. There are seven large organizations working officially in the war zone. Besides the two just mentioned the Salvation Army, the Knights of Columbus, the Jewish Welfare Board, the American Library Association and the Young Women's Christian Association are doing excellent work. Among the seven our soldiers get about all the little food luxuries they need.

Soldiers are omniverous candy eaters, and they deserve all the candy they want. But ship space is precious. It is so precious that the War Department had to deprive us of the great privilege of sending packages to our sons. Only essentials, asked for by the soldiers and approved by their officers, can be shipped now.

The Y. M. C. A. has to work hard to keep its canteens supplied, for not only is shipping space limited, but the railroads all over France are congested with freight. The Red Cross uses its own motor-trucks except for long hauls. So it seems a real duty to ship as little as possible overseas, and to distribute as much as possible through one of the seven official organizations.

That is the economical way, and the only way in which the cost of distributing can be kept down. Every separate society means more overhead charges.

But what becomes of individual effort? it is suggested. We want to do something more than give money. We want to give personal service. Of course. I should like to see women in the United States in the same close personal touch with the government and with the army and navy as the women of England are. I should like to see over here an organization of women like the British Women's Army Auxiliary Corps, the "Wacks" as they are called. These women are regularly enlisted members of the army. They sign up for the duration of the war, they are under the war ministry, they are subject to discipline, they have their own officers, a uniform, they live in barracks and they are paid by the government.

The "Wacks" are organized to take the places of men who are needed to fight. They do all kinds of clerical work, they cook, wait on table at officers' mess, they have charge of supplies, they have almost entirely taken over the signal branch, telephoning and telegraphing and the like. There really seems to be little that the "Wacks" haven't taken over in the way of civilian tasks. They even assist the veterinarians in taking care of sick and wounded horses and mules.

There are about twenty thousand women in this branch of the British service. Some of them work in Great Britain and others in France. Often they have served under fire, and always with great bravery. The telephone and telegraph operators have been cited for coolness and devotion to duty under shell fire and air raids. Great Britain is proud of her Women's Auxiliary Army.

She is proud also of the Women's Royal Naval Service, known as the "Wrens," of the great land army of women who work on farms and help feed the country and the army in France. Altogether there are over a million women in Great Britain who have signed up for government controlled war work.

I talked with General Pershing about the possibility of organizing women in America to release men for the trenches. I told him that it distressed me to see men in uniform working at card indexes, sorting mail, pounding typewriters and attending to telephones. He said that it was only a question of time before some of this work, at least, would be taken over by women.

"I know that we shall have to have women telephone operators," said the commander. And within a few months the first women telephonists were actually in France.

General Pershing told me at the close of our conversation that he should, if consulted, recommend that the work of our women be begun at home, in the cantonments. That strikes me as an excellent idea.

Women ought to be signed up for clerical work, garden work and especially for housekeeping work in all the cantonments. A uniform is absolutely necessary, and the women should be officered and disciplined by women. They should take over most tasks not actually military, thus releasing officers and men to drill. In this way the work of speeding up a huge army would be greatly accelerated.

Our army in the cantonments and in the field abroad is very well fed, but there is no standard which has to be maintained in all the regiments. If a company has a good mess sergeant the food is good, well selected, well cooked and served. If it has a poor mess sergeant the food is abundant but not well cooked or served.

If the officers of a regiment are as zealous, thoughtful and resourceful as they ought to be the men are as well taken care of as they would be at home. I have in mind as a model officer a young first lieutenant, a Yale man, in command of a company of negro stevedores, at one of the great ports which we are using in France.

These men were all from the cotton fields of Georgia and Alabama and the levees of the lower Mississippi. They were magnificent physical specimens, but fully seventy-five per cent. were illiterate. Some officers would have looked upon them as animals only fit to work. But this officer was a real person, and to him each stevedore was an individual.

He made out of scanty materials a comfortable, sanitary, up-to-date camp for his regiment. He had a bath house and a swimming pool, a laundry, a big, cool, screened kitchen, a club for officers and a sitting-room for the men. He had a cooking squad that was the envy of the neighborhood and meals that were famous for miles around.

He told me how he did it. He said that he felt sure that among all those negroes there must be a lot of individual talent, and he went to work to find it. He found one man who was a soup and meat cook when he was not a cotton picker, and this man was made soup and meat cook. He found another cook to whom he entrusted the vegetables. Another man was taught in the town to cook desserts and pastry.

When spring came this resourceful young lieutenant planted a garden, detaching certain men from their stevedoring long enough to spade, cultivate and plant. He had one of the happiest, healthiest, most efficient working forces I saw in France. Why? Because he possessed many of the housekeeping instincts of a woman.

Not all, perhaps not many, officers in our army have housekeeping instincts, nor have they time to do what this young Yale man did. The housekeeping work of the army ought to a very great extent be in the hands of women. It is the work they know how to do. It is important, and women would be as proud to succeed in it as the soldiers are to win victories.

I would not like to be interpreted as being against all small organizations for war work. Many of the existing ones are doing good work. I know that all women can not leave their homes for regular work in any organization. But unless some miracle ends this war within a year, I hope to see a great army of American women enlisted like soldiers, for the duration of hostilities uniformed and paid workers behind the battle line here and in France, Italy, and wherever else the war calls for workers.

---

# CHAPTER XXVIII
# THE DARK OCEAN LANES

IN THE quiet little hotel which is my home when I am on this side of the Atlantic, there have been staying until recently a group of army nurses. There were about one hundred and thirty of these nurses, fine, strong, skilled women, and they were in New York on their way to France.

They didn't know where they were to be stationed. They were a California nursing unit and their goal was a base hospital—but in what part of France the base hospital was to be located, they knew no more than I did.

All they knew was that they were anxious to be off. They were as eager to get to work in that hospital as our soldiers are to get to the front. They fretted at the delay, and they asked me a thousand questions about France, about the medical service corps, about the hospitals. Soon after their arrival at the Atlantic coast the German submarines made their sudden, savage attacks on American shipping. American waters were reported full of these vipers of the sea.

They were said by some to be accompanied by a "mother ship" which would keep them supplied for an indefinite stay. There was talk of a possible base in Mexico from which whole fleets of U-boats would come and go. Did all this have the slightest effect on those nurses or on their eagerness to sail? Not a bit of it. They simply said, wouldn't it be the limit if Secretary Daniels stopped all sailings? But of course he wouldn't.

One morning I opened my door and saw a group of these California nurses standing guard over an enormous pile of hand luggage, suit-cases, satchels and hold-alls. The women greeted me with broad smiles.

"Well," I said, "you look as if you had packed all your troubles in your old kit bags."

"We have," they chorused. "Nobody's got a trouble in the world. We sail 'from an Atlantic port' this afternoon!"

Right out into the submarines. Across three thousand miles of peril. Into the unknown. Without a fear. This is not exactly what the war lords planned when they sent their biggest submarines to blockade the American coast. They did not hope, of course, to stop all shipping from this side. But they undoubtedly counted on terrorizing the American people, especially the women.

Not even the inflated German mind conceived the notion that their submarines would prevent the sailing of army transports. But we can easily imagine the kaiser and his councilors reasoning that the mothers and fathers and wives of the soldiers would be so terrified that there would be trouble in the United States, trouble for President Wilson and Congress. Riots in the streets, maybe. Breakdown of American morale. They must have licked their lips at the thought.

The German psychology has been curiously twisted before on this terror question, but it persists in spite of the fact that nothing they have done in this war, not even the ultimate horrors they committed in Belgium, Serbia and Armenia, ever frightened anybody except the immediate victims. The nations that are bent on crushing out the authors of horror have never been terrorized.

Nevertheless I know that the mothers and fathers and wives of soldiers, and the immediate relatives of trained nurses who are crossing the seas in these perilous times, must suffer great anxiety. Perhaps it may give them a little comfort to know that the travelers suffer less fear than they do. Perhaps they might like to know what a sea voyage is really like in war time. Some know, for they have crossed. The majority, however, have not.

I have crossed the Atlantic four times since we entered the war, twice in a neutral boat, once in an American, and once in a French boat. The first two voyages scarcely count because the lane through which we traveled was out of the submarine zone. Making due allowances for the shifting of the zone, and for the boche's criminal practise of sinking neutral boats "by mistake," our steamer was lighted up at night like Coney Island, and her name and nationality was displayed on both sides of the hull in letters which could be read at a great distance.

In sharp contrast, the American and French boats were kept as dark as pockets all the way over. They were camouflaged in a manner that made me laugh when I went aboard. All portholes were painted a dark green, and they were locked every day at sundown. No lights were shown, and travelers were strictly forbidden after dark to smoke or to light a match on deck.

Of course, there was no music, no band on board. No loud noise of any kind was permitted. The American boat was peculiarly constructed, in that the passageways leading to the main gangway had portholes and doors looking out on deck. Because of the necessity of showing no lights these passageways were inky dark at night. When we went down to dinner we found our way by taking hold of a rope stretched from one end of the passageway to the companion and then down to the dining saloon.

The first thing that happens on a voyage nowadays is a life-boat drill. A typewritten list is posted prominently, giving each passenger's life-boat assignment. At the designated hour, shortly after sailing, the passengers all put on life preservers and report at the life-boat station to which they have been directed. A ship's company just now is overwhelmingly masculine, and when all passengers are assembled the women find that there are about two of them to each life-boat, and that their boats are generally filled with responsible men and commanded by an officer.

The officer in command of the life-boat visits each boat station and calls the roll to make sure that no one has failed to attend the drill. The officer makes a speech at each station, telling the passengers exactly what to do if the danger signal is sounded. They must immediately make for their assigned places, fastening on their life belts as they go. The sailors assigned to the various boats will be the first to arrive, and they know their duties. As for the passengers, the women are to get into the boats before the men. When all are in their seats the boat will be lowered.

You get into the habit of lingering near your assigned life-boat. The locality has a homelike feel. You time yourself to see how long it takes to get from your stateroom to the life-boat, and it gives a certain confidence to learn that you can easily make it in two or three minutes without running.

At night you put your warmest clothes where you can get into them quickly. Your life belt is always where you can grasp it in a second. When you approach the danger zone the life belt is never out of sight. It hangs on the arm of your steamer chair, it goes to the table with you. Soldiers, officers, nurses and Red Cross members are required to wear their life belts all the time while in the zone.

No fear enters into these things. Nobody shows fear, nor do I think that many feel fear. The vision of sudden death is present, but only as a mental conception. Like being at the front. One gets used to it.

On my American boat there was a very fine young naval officer in command of as splendid a gun crew as you would care to see. The ship was mounted with eight guns, and one day in mid-ocean we had a gun drill. The gunners, who had never left a single piece unmanned for a minute, night or day, now had an opportunity to show the passengers that they could shoot as well as they could keep guard.

A target hardly larger than the periscope of a submarine was nailed to an empty barrel and thrown overboard. When it was distant a quarter of a mile, and only faintly to be seen by unpractised eyes, the commander gave the word and the six-inch guns forward blazed away at it. The ship meanwhile was zigzagging just as she would in a real submarine attack. In a minute or two this brought the aft guns into play. One after another they flashed and roared; and although the target was not struck at the first shots, every shell fell near enough to have struck the U-boat had the target been its periscope.

The firing kept up for twenty minutes or more, the boat continuing its gyrations the while, then she settled down to her steady gait, and the commander came in for felicitations.

"That zigzag the captain has figured out," he said, modestly ignoring his own part in the performance, "would make a submarine crew cross-eyed trying to follow it."

Three days before we reached the British shores both the captain and the commander vanished from sight. They never came into the dining saloon again during the voyage. They spent their time on the bridge tirelessly watching. Up in the crow's nest two sailors also watched. With strong glasses they swept the horizon and never ceased.

The life-boats which hitherto had been swung high up and level with the boat deck, now were lowered to the level of the promenade deck. Everything was in readiness. Far out across the gray and tumbling sea the early dawn had seen the approach of two American destroyers, the swiftest, slimmest, smartest little craft afloat. It is no secret that these American destroyers are and have for some time been patrolling British waters, and magnificent work they have done.

Exactly how many submarines our little destroyers have sent to the bottom has not been given out, but Mr. Lloyd George has more than once in the House of Commons reported that the American boats were having continuous successes.

All the rest of the way those two swift destroyers convoyed us. They swept in great circles all around us. They plowed through the waves like dolphins, the water sometimes completely engulfing them. They never rested, and the passengers sat all day and watched them with fascinated eyes. Nothing could happen with those destroyers at hand.

Such is the sea voyage on which our sons and our daughters are traveling in these times of great peril and uncertainty. As far as it is humanly possible their lives are safeguarded against the enemy. There is little difference in the precautions taken to defend the transports. That each ship has traveled back and forth so many times in safety is one of the marvels of the war.

To sink an American transport with several thousand soldiers on board, any U-boat commander in the Germany navy would almost barter his chances in the next world. Can you imagine to what fame he would spring overnight? They would have to invent a new decoration to express the kaiser's gratitude—his and Gott's. But nobody has won that decoration yet, and nobody stands much chance of winning it, if only the American father and mother keep cool and stand by their government.

We have sent over, Secretary Baker told us in early July, more than a million soldiers, and we have lost less than three hundred men at sea. Think of it! The sea at that rate, even now, with U-boats on both sides of the Atlantic, is safer to cross than Broadway and Forty-second Street. Shall we keep it safe? Or shall we do what the kaiser is probably praying for every day of his life? Shall we please him, help him, by demanding that some of those destroyers be sent home to guard our shores? Never, while we keep our intelligence.

# CHAPTER XXIX
# CLEMENCEAU THE TIGER

IT MUST be plain to everybody, even to the people of the German empire and her vassal states, that the allies will certainly win the war. The only thing that could possibly alter that fact would be for one of the great powers, England, France or the United States, to make a very serious political blunder. We need not be afraid now that such a thing will happen. We know that President Wilson will stand firmly by the policies which have brought him fame and gratitude throughout the civilized world.

Great Britain has had her worst political crisis, and she has survived it. We trust David Lloyd George to work wholeheartedly with Woodrow Wilson for a fight to the finish with German militarism. But what of France? What manner of man is at the helm in the French capital? What about Clemenceau?

All I knew about Clemenceau, when I went to France last January, was that he was the editor of a newspaper which seemed to attack everybody in the French government, and which was frequently suppressed by the censor. I had never seen a copy of the paper. I knew that Clemenceau had had a long political career, had been a member of the French Senate, and also of the Chamber of Deputies, which corresponds to our House of Representatives. For a brief period also he was prime minister.

Always Clemenceau appeared to be opposing something. I thought of him as a firebrand with a talent for writing ironic newspaper articles. Therefore, when I reached Paris, when I began to read the French papers and found them filled with praises of a man they had previously denounced as a Judas; when I heard the most conservative people speak of him as the savior of France, I was filled with curiosity. I began to ask everybody to tell me all about Clemenceau.

To see him was difficult. To interview him an impossibility. He spends half his time at the front, and the other half working. Rarely did he find time to visit the Chamber of Deputies. His speeches came at rare intervals, and were never announced beforehand. So the foreign office informed me.

The best I could do was to sit down with people who knew the prime minister and get from them the extraordinary history of the man. Added to that I followed day by day in the newspapers the amazing progress of his policies announced last November when he took office.

"You ask my war aims?" he said to the Chamber. "I have only one—to win."

Part of the programme of winning the war was the suppression of the tribe of traitors and defeatists that disgraced the name of France. These, including the unspeakable Bolo and the former minister, Caillaux, Clemenceau had fiercely attacked in his newspaper.

When he told the Chamber that he intended to push the prosecution of the accused men to the finish, some one called out unbelievingly, "What! Caillaux?" naming the man who wielded immense power, and who, while Clemenceau was making his speech of acceptance, was seated in the Chamber a few feet from the tribune, a cynical smile on his lips.

Thus challenged, Clemenceau paused just long enough to turn and fix his blazing black eyes on the man he had so often accused. He did not say a word. He just looked. Turning furiously red, Caillaux half rose from his seat. Clemenceau's fierce eyes bored him through, and, try as he might, Caillaux could not return the gaze. He sank in his seat with averted head.

Turning once more to the deputies Clemenceau said simply that as a newspaper man he mentioned names, but as premier he would merely deal with indicted criminals.

He has dealt with them. Bolo has been executed. Almereyda, one of the worst of the lot, died a violent death in prison, Duval followed Bolo to the fatal glade in the Park of Vincennes, Humbert was exiled and Caillaux is in prison with the strongest possible prospect of being shot as a traitor. A whole raft of smaller treason mongers have received prison terms.

Clemenceau is doing what the former governments seemed to find impossible. He has adjourned politics. And when I found that out I understood why this man, the "Tiger," as he is styled, is also called the savior of France. For France has been cursed with politics and politicians, and it is no affront to the most universally loved and admired of all nations to make that admission.

I have no intention of trying to explain the political parties of France, or the minute shades of opinion that separate them. The Chamber of Deputies has a right, or conservative, a left, or radical, and a center. But every one of the three has a right, left and center, and each one of the subdivisions seems to have. This explains why France, or at least Paris, has more newspapers than any place in the world.

Scores of newspapers are displayed on the news-stands, and there are some that are not displayed at all, but are circulated none the less. Most of these papers have only four pages and some have only two. They are supported not by subscriptions or sales, much less by advertising. The political group which each represents does the supporting.

With all these warring political parties represented in the Chamber of Deputies, it is a wonder that anything in the way of legislation is effected. But the French people managed very well, until the war. Then it was time to call a truce. But no prime minister before Clemenceau was able to bring about a truce.

Clemenceau, who had been out of office for some years, thundered away in his paper, *L'Homme Libre*, the *Free Man*, excoriating, abusing, calling down invectives on all party leaders alike. The mildest term he applied to President Poincaré was Nero. The censor suppressed one issue of the *Free Man* cutting out everything in it except the head-lines. Clemenceau changed the name of his paper to the *Man in Chains*. The censor ignored him for a time and he changed it again to the *Man Less Chained*.

Everybody read the paper, because it was so brilliantly written, especially the two columns of invective which Clemenceau signed every day. Nevertheless, it was a scandal. Nobody was spared. The "Tiger" respected nor wealth nor power.

Things were at a troublous pass in France during the year 1917. The war did not approach an end. There was a serious shortage of fuel. Agricultural affairs were in a tangle. Russia, which owed France vast sums of money, had collapsed. Traitors were abroad in the land. While the real France fought gloriously, immortally at Verdun, and at Ypres, the politicians in the capital wrangled the hours away.

People began to say, "We must have a strong government. There must be unity. Who is the man to give it to us?" One after another man they tried, splendid men. Ribot, the diplomat, the grand old aristocrat, who could talk familiarly with kings, the man who had made the Franco-Russian alliance. Painlevé, the intellectual, one of the greatest mathematicians in Europe. Other statesmen. One by one they had fallen. Clemenceau was usually responsible for their fall. He kept after them until they got too unpopular to last. He is said, in the course of his entire career, to have wrecked sixteen ministries and he certainly removed one president.

People began to say: "That man Clemenceau, that 'Tiger,' who has been such a firebrand, such a thorn in the side of all the governments, that man has usually been right in his judgments. He was right about Salonica. We should never have sent General Sarrail there. He was needed for France. Clemenceau said so at the time, and he was right.

"He was right about Bolo, too. He probably knew what he was talking about when he accused Caillaux of trying to persuade Italy to sue for a separate peace with Germany. He was right when he said there ought to be a generalissimo at the head of the allied armies. Nobody, not even his worst enemies, ever accused the 'Tiger' of being anything but a good patriot. Why, he is the biggest and most single-minded patriot in France. What if we had to have Clemenceau for prime minister?"

At first the idea was laughed at. Then it was discussed, but then everybody said: "It can't be done. The Unified Socialists have declared against him in advance. Poincaré may nominate him, for he is big enough to forget that he was called a Nero, but without the vote of the Unified Socialists the Chamber of Deputies can not confirm any nomination." The Unified Socialists, it seems, is a party that hangs together better than some of the other radical groups.

Last November there was a real crisis in France. No use going into details now, because it is past. But when the crisis was at its height the people discovered that Clemenceau was not a firebrand after all. He was the voice of France.

His opposition had almost always been opposition to hypocrisy and incompetence. His fiery invective was fierce common sense, the common sense of the good, brave, clear-visioned French mind. Here, at least, was a man, not a politician. The Unified Socialists alone clung to their opposition, confident that they could block Clemenceau's appointment. They had blocked both Ribot and Painlevé in their efforts to form ministries. They were ready to keep Clemenceau from office.

Nevertheless, Poincaré sent for Clemenceau and asked him to become prime minister. He accepted bruskly, appealed to the Chamber of Deputies in a speech full of patriotism and intelligent statements of facts. He was accepted as prime minister by every vote in the house except the fifty Unified Socialists and fifteen extreme radicals. The vote stood four hundred and eighteen to sixty-five.

Clemenceau formed a cabinet which rather astonished the French at first. He appointed two men who were not even members of the Chamber of Deputies. He included two of his old associates of former days who had been almost as unpopular as himself. The newspapers, while speaking moderately of all this, accused Clemenceau of being a dictator. "He rules with a rod of iron," they complained. "He won't let his ministers mention the word peace in his presence. He works everybody to death."

This old man of seventy-six is a fiend for work. He once said that one reason he wrecked those ministries was because they wasted so much time. He opened the allied conference at Versailles with the shortest speech on record. "Gentlemen, we are here to work. Let us work." The speech is shorter still when it is turned into French.

Soon most of the newspapers were supporting the prime minister. He may have been a dictator, but he got results. He took treason by the throat and strangled it. He took hold of the army and strengthened it. At least three times a week he motors to the front, going so close to the firing line that several times he has been in great danger, and once he narrowly escaped being captured by a German patrol.

If that patrol had captured Clemenceau the kaiser would have issued a new medal and had all the church bells in the empire rung, for the prime minister is, of all Frenchmen, the most feared and hated by Germany.

He has always seen through the Germans. His newspaper has exposed their intrigues time out of mind. About ten years ago the Germans tried to seduce France into a huge colonial expansion scheme, and if they had succeeded France and Great Britain might have become hopelessly involved.

That was one of Germany's objects. Another was to take France's mind off Alsace-Lorraine. Jules Ferry, then prime minister, fell into the trap, but not so Clemenceau. He denounced Ferry's colonial policy, called it by its right name, German intrigue, so tigerishly and so long, that the people woke up and Ferry went out of office.

Once when Clemenceau was prime minister before, the German government took offense at something that was said or done to one of its consuls in Morocco. The chancellor sent for the French ambassador in Berlin and demanded an apology. If it were not quickly forthcoming the German ambassador at Paris would be recalled. When this was transmitted to Clemenceau he sent for the German ambassador. He told him without any preamble that there would be no apology. "If you want your passports they are ready for you," he added. Germany backed down.

Clemenceau's diplomacy is like that. When the Austrian premier dared to put forth the slander that Clemenceau had sent a peace emissary to him the public clamored for a statement. The prime minister, on his way to the front, paused long enough to say over his shoulder to the interviewers: "Count Czernin lies." And so it proved.

The greatest thing that Clemenceau has done was to unite the allied armies under a generalissimo. President Wilson wanted it done long ago. The wisest among the English wanted it done. But there were difficulties that seemed insuperable. Then came the almost fatal break in the British line last March. Clemenceau rushed up to the front, and what he said there has never been revealed. But it was to the point, and it smashed all the insuperable obstacles at one blow. Foch took command. The disaster was averted.

"I am not old," said Clemenceau humorously to a friend. "I am just aged." That is true. At a time when most men are ready to retire he is crowning his life's work. He is the most thoroughly alive man in France and one of the greatest men in the world.

His newspaper, again *L'Homme Libre*, is still published, but Clemenceau's name appears merely as founder. It is still a good newspaper, better in some respects than before, because one of the first things that Clemenceau did after taking office was to trim the censorship down to zero. They have a fairly free press in France now.

---

# CHAPTER XXX
# FROM ALL FOES, FOREIGN OR DOMESTIC

NO STATESMAN is so great that he is admired and supported by his entire community. Monsieur Clemenceau, the splendid prime minister of France, who has done so much in a few short months to unify his nation and to bring the allied armies together under one commander-in-chief, is no exception to the rule. He has with him in the Chamber of Deputies the solid vote of the right and center, the conservative and moderate vote, and he has also some of the left or radical vote. He is opposed by the radical socialists only.

Some of the radicals with whom I talked in France urged me, if I were to understand the French mind, to see and talk with the leader of the opposition, Albert Thomas. So one morning I went, by appointment, to the modest apartment in the neighborhood of the Chamber of Deputies which is the home of Monsieur Thomas, and the center of activities of the radical socialists of France.

Accompanying me was Mademoiselle St. René Taillandier of the French foreign office, a young woman of exceptional intellect and an accomplished linguist. Speaking English as well as her native French, Mademoiselle St. René Taillandier agreed to go with me to interview Monsieur Thomas, lest any shade of meaning in what he said to me might be lost.

Monsieur Thomas speaks no English, and I, of course, have an imperfect knowledge of French. Whenever I failed to understand some idiom or figure of speech I halted the conversation until it could be interpreted into English.

I wanted to be fair to Monsieur Thomas and his political group. My previously conceived admiration for Clemenceau made me all the more anxious to understand exactly why he was so vigorously opposed. We talked for nearly an hour, and when I was down in the street again, walking along the glittering Seine, I said to my friend: "We have them like that in the United States, honest, sincere, intelligent idealists; with blinders on."

Judging from what I saw and heard in the apartment of Monsieur Albert Thomas that morning, France must have a considerable group of such idealists. We were early for our appointment and waited for ten minutes in the reception room, which was more like an office, with a long table strewn with socialist literature and propaganda pamphlets, and around the walls a row of stiff cane seated chairs.

A little girl in a black cambric pinafore attended the door, which frequently opened to admit more visitors. During my talk with Monsieur Thomas the same little girl appeared half a dozen times bearing cards and notes. There is no doubt that Monsieur Thomas is the leader of a strong group.

The head of the radical socialists in France is a man of forty something, short, thickset, with blue, intelligent eyes behind steel rimmed spectacles. He has rather long brown hair, a beard of a lighter shade of brown.

His speech is quick and animated, with a little too much oratory in it. Every question I asked him was answered by a speech. It made me think of Gladstone of whom Queen Victoria said: "He addresses me as if I were a public meeting."

I asked Monsieur Thomas to tell me the spirit of the French working people during the war. Were they wholeheartedly patriotic, or was there any of the industrial unrest that had made itself felt in England.

"Our French working class is more stable than the British," he replied. "Every French man and woman worthy of the name wants the allies to win the war. In the Chamber of Deputies there have been only three men who have not shown themselves genuinely patriotic.

"Those three went to Switzerland and discussed the war with certain Germans. Their act was denounced by all other socialists as well as by the bourgeois deputies. The men have absolutely no following."

"Is the French working class solidly socialist, or has it a majority of socialists?"

"It has not a majority in numbers, but the socialist element is very powerful, much more powerful than surface indications show. In time of strikes the party always wields great influence. It is impossible for a stranger to understand the extent of socialist opinion throughout France. Reading the newspapers would not convey the facts to the stranger, because unfortunately the press and the people here are not together."

"Is your socialism revolutionary?" I asked.

"No, it is more philosophical than revolutionary," was the reply. "The opinions of your President Wilson are almost exactly ours. His war aims as stated by him find absolute echo in the French popular mind. Much more so than in the mind of the government." This with a flash and a gesture that spelled "Clemenceau" very clearly.

"We are not Bolsheviki, we are French," he added with emphasis.

"I wish you would explain to me, if you are solidly in favor of a peace with victory for the allies, why your group, and especially you as leader, wanted to go to the Stockholm conference and discuss peace without victory with the Germans."

Monsieur Thomas demurred a little at my way of putting the question, and right here I began to notice the blinders.

"It is true that I was and am warmly in favor of the Stockholm conference," he began. "I regret very much that Mr. Gompers and the American Federation of Labor have misunderstood my attitude and my object in wanting to meet in Stockholm representatives of the workers of all nations. They seem to think that my object was to fraternize with the Germans. Not at all. My object was to tell the whole German people the allies' war aims, and their stated terms of peace.

"The German people do not know these aims. The imperial government keeps the people in ignorance. The press censorship is so complete that the real terms on which we are willing to make peace have never been published. We can not get at the German people through their newspapers.

"We could have talked to them through the Stockholm conference, because even the censored press would have published the proceedings of that conference. The Germans then would have known the truth."

"What makes you think that the censored press of Germany would have been permitted to publish the proceedings of the Stockholm conference?" I asked. "It was not permitted to publish the war aims speeches of President Wilson or Mr. Lloyd George."

"Why," exclaimed Monsieur Thomas, with what appeared to me a childish innocence, "their own loyal Germans would have attended as delegates, and of course the people would insist on hearing their reports.

"Don't misunderstand me," he said. "I admit that such a conference with the enemy, at a time when the allied armies are engaged in killing that same enemy on the battle-field, would be morally and sentimentally a grave thing. But I am certain that the advantages would have outweighed the disadvantages. All the French socialists, except a group on the right, agree with my point of view.

"After the war the working classes in all the countries will have to stand together, will have to have a common programme, that they may force their point of view on the governments. The Stockholm conference would have furthered that solidarity. I regret that the American working class can not see that."

I turned the question to the Russian collapse.

"Ah, Russia, a great mystery, is it not? When you think she is about to commit a treachery you see a Brousiloff offensive. When you think she is about to be sublime you behold the Brest-Litovsk surrender. Anarchy! But Russia is too great to fall permanently.

"Why are not France and America there now, helping poor, wounded Russia? All we do is to send a message to the Moscow soviet: 'Russia will emerge.' *Mon Dieu!*"

"To whom would you offer your help, Lenine and Trotzky?" I asked. "Do you think that we can help the Russian people through men who are daily delivering them piecemeal to the Germans?"

"Oh, I do not think Lenine and Trotzky are exactly German agents, although it is evident that they took German money," was the extraordinary reply. "They are not traitors, they are fanatics. They see nothing except their propaganda. Here was money offered them, money they needed for their propaganda. German money—true, but what of it? They would take any money!"

Monsieur Albert Thomas evidently could not see that men who would take German money were incapable of being honest leaders, sincere prophets, or anything in the world but liars, thieves and traitors. No man can exist half crook, half honest.

"They see nothing but their propaganda." That is a perfect description of Monsieur Albert Thomas and all the other misguided idealists who walk with blinders obscuring their eyes. They think and talk as though unaware that the world around them was in flames.

On a battle-front of seventy-five miles our allied soldiers are enduring such hardships, are performing such miracles of labor, are suffering such wounds, such horrible mutilations, that no imagination can compass the facts. Every day some of these heroic men give their blood, their beautiful young lives for the freedom of the world.

They die for our liberty without a murmur. And while they are suffering and dying, a whole section of the community in every allied country continues to ignore them for one or another fatuous dream.

In France when these dreamers beat at the Chamber of Deputies to be allowed to go to Stockholm, Clemenceau answered them: "I understand your idealism, and I share it. But where we differ is that I am under no illusion regarding the reality of facts."

The only important fact in the world is that we are fighting the greatest war in history, "in order that government of the people, for the people, and by the people shall not perish from the earth." Nothing else matters. Nothing.

Every other question is a side issue, something to be considered and acted upon after we have won the war.

In this country we have our Bolsheviki who would take advantage of the fact that our best beloved, our sons, are fighting, giving their lives in a far land, to seize power for their "class." We have fanatics whose paranoia finds expression in "radical" magazines. We have propagandists who find supreme satisfaction in going around the country making defeatist speeches, and we have a public which exclaims in horror when one of these talkers is arrested and given a well-merited prison sentence.

We have lawmakers, men in Congress, whose devotion to their propaganda is so limitless that they are willing to risk losing army appropriations, delaying the progress of the war, in order to hasten a little the prohibition campaign.

We have theorists who can not think very much about the war because they are so occupied with getting on good terms again with a people who never were honestly on good terms with anybody except themselves. After all these years of slaughter these theorists would smilingly get together with the men who willed the slaughter and talk about a league of nations, a society to abolish war.

"A league of nations!" exclaimed Clemenceau to the Unified Socialists of France, led by Albert Thomas. "What will a league of nations mean without Germany? I for one will not let Germany in. You would do so, and on what guarantees? Ask Belgium!"

What are we Americans, those of us who walk without blinders, who see and know the awful realities of the hour, going to do about the class fanatics, propagandists, egotist individualists, the sentimental theorists, big and little? They are traitors to the world that is struggling to be free. Whether they know it or not, they are traitors. They fight side by side with Attila.

Rather, they are the camp followers of the Hun, for they rarely do any fighting. When justice overtakes them they nearly always throw up their hands and cry "Kamerad." They almost invariably claim that they didn't mean to be disloyal.

The only thing to do with these people is to snatch the blinders from their eyes and make them look at the reality of a world at righteous war. As soon as one defeatist comes within the law, seize him, imprison him. Whether he is an I. W. W. criminal or a university professor, or even a United States senator. Keep on doing it. Treat women exactly as the men are treated. It wouldn't take long before the blinders would begin to fall without assistance.

# CHAPTER XXXI
## LAFAYETTE, WE'RE HERE

ONE of the great moments of this war was when General Pershing, newly arrived in France, was escorted in state to the tomb of the man who, in his ardent youth, left the most luxurious court in Europe, crossed the seas and offered his sword to George Washington.

The President of the French republic, the commander of the French army, with other dignitaries of the state and army, were in that escorting party, and when they approached the tomb they paused in silence, with bared heads, to hear what General Pershing should say. They expected a formal speech, but I do not think General Pershing could have made a speech just then. What he felt was too deep and too moving. His hand touched the hilt of his sword and then the hand went out toward the marble, and General Pershing said simply:

"Lafayette, we're here."

After the passing of a hundred and forty years we are in France to pay our debt, to offer our sword, the sword of America, to the cause of liberty. Whoever says we are fighting a profiteers' war or a politicians' war utters a lying slander. Whoever intimates that we shall ever sheathe the sword of America until the war is won, and the world is safe, simply does not know the facts, nor the temper of our army.

To make the world safe for democracy. That phrase has been repeated so many times that it has become almost a colloquialism. It is used in jest sometimes. But it is written on the hearts of the millions of men who have gone out to die, if need be, to make that dream a reality.

Whatever confusion of thought there may have been in the minds of the first armies that rushed out against the German invasion, there is no confusion or misunderstanding in the minds of those who fight to-day. The Belgians and the French fought first to save their homes. The British fought because they knew that their homes would next be endangered. The Russians and the Italians fought because they were attacked.

No doubt there was in the consciousness of some European statesmen the hope of territorial gains, or diplomatic advantages to follow after an allied victory. But that has all vanished now, drowned in the blood of the brave at Malines, Louvain, the Marne, Verdun, Rheims, Cantigny, Château Thierry, St. Michiel. Europe, except that part of it still ruled by Attila and his slaves, has purged itself of the old statesmanship, the old sinuous, scheming diplomacy.

There will never be any more Metternichs, or Talleyrands or Castlereaghs, never any more secret agreements between kings and statesmen. The old order has perished and now we have freemen fighting under leaders like Wilson, Lloyd George, Clemenceau, to make the world free.

The hope of the toiling masses all over the world, the vision of seers and prophets and poets since the dawn of time; the dreams dreamed in garrets, in city slums, in the snows of Siberia, on gallows high, on the sacred cross. The world set free. Free from the oppression of tyrants claiming divine rights; free from the cold exploitation of privilege; free from poverty and all the crime and prostitution and death that rise like a hideous miasma from the mire of poverty; free from war!

That is the free world for which our sons have crossed the seas to fight. That is the freedom for which almost every country in the world has united against the only remaining countries that do not want it, Germany, Austria, Turkey, Bulgaria.

In these pages I have tried to tell America, and especially the mothers of American soldiers, the meaning of the war, as it was shown to me over there. I have tried to picture to them how their sons are preparing to take their part in the war. How they are growing up to their task, how they are building the strong structure of an army, how they are laying the foundation of true internationalism, how we through our army are forming with the democratic peoples of the world a holy alliance much greater and more permanent than anything kings or statesmen ever planned.

When this is being written the year is barely finished that saw the first American transports sail for France. Yet over hundreds of miles of territory behind the battle lines our men, with hard and grueling labor, have built the industrial forts that in this practical age are necessary to an army's life. They have established a base of supplies for millions of fighting men. They have built barracks, airdromes, hospitals, warehouses, factories and repair shops.

They have laid railroads, built wharves, dredged a great river. They have done more, our men, than dig themselves in trenches over there. They have shown Europe and the world the true heart and metal of America. What they have built will remain a monument for generations to point to and admire.

In Paris there stands a noble monument to our Washington, and at no great distance there is another to the rugged giant Abraham Lincoln. Each February the French people go and lay wreaths on these monuments. For years they have done this, and since April 6, 1917, they have kept their colors entwined with ours there.

Those statues are symbols of the historic friendship of France and America. I like to think that after the war, when great ships sail out of an ancient port of France, the sailors will remember that once they had to wait for the highest tide, but that American brawn and engineering skill scooped out the centuries of sand and silt that their biggest transports might pass with ease.

I like to believe that France will grow and prosper because of the railroads we laid down, the wharves and warehouses we built. Not in a spirit of boastfulness, but of love and gratitude do I wish that France may benefit from the things we have created on her soil.

I like also to think that the France of to-morrow, and the Belgium which will be reborn, will be healthier, happier, stronger of mind and soul for the work of our Red Cross, for all the relief and succor we have been able to send there. They will never forget, those martyred Belgians, those hard pressed French. Our troops never pass through a village, our flag never appears that the children in the street fail to salute.

Once they had reason to believe, those brave allies in Europe, that we were merely generous of money, that we were willing to give only out of our overflowing pockets. But since we began to give our men they think otherwise. They know now that everything we have, everything we are, is pledged to the fight against tyranny and the world's woe.

This spring and summer will see the preliminary work of building an army well nigh completed, and the men who have been handling picks and shovels, those who have been learning the war game, the men in camps and army schools will be ready to fight. Already they have won their spurs in several fierce engagements, and not yet has any fight of theirs been lost. Already American soldiers are in Lorraine and Alsace, fighting on what Germany calls her soil, but which will never be hers, even in name, again.

Can you imagine the wild joy, the renewed hope, the quickened spirit that fills the hearts of the men who have been fighting for nearly four years? Against terrible odds, against one ally which German cunning poisoned to death, almost against hope our allies have fought. Thank heaven that we came up in time.

There is one question every returned correspondent is asked, and the question has been put to me but I have never answered it. When will the war end? I am going to answer it now. Not in terms of years, because I, no more than the greatest general, can do that. The war is going to end when it is won. Not a day, not an hour before. Much fighting, horrible suffering, enormous sacrifice lie between us and victory, but victory is sure.

We shall lose thousands, hundreds of thousands, it may be. But for every American soldier that falls eight Germans will die, be sure of that. The only army in the world that is absolutely fresh and untired is the American army. Our men will tire, but before they do all the Germans left alive will be exhausted.

The pæan sung by William the accursed to glorify the thirtieth anniversary of his succession to the throne of the Hohenzollerns is the last one he will ever sing. The first battle in France by an American division sealed the doom of the Hohenzollerns. It was the beginning of the last act of the world's bloodiest drama.

Lafayette, we're here. The countrymen of Washington and Lincoln could not keep out of this fight. We shall never stop coming, never stop fighting until the war to free the world is won. France, Italy, Belgium, Russia, wherever the red tide leads take our sons. Spare us all useless sacrifices, for they are very dear to us, those young, bright lives.

But take them, take them all if need be, leave this generation wholly bereft and mourning, rather than surrender to the hordes of Attila. Better for us any sacrifice of blood and tears than to lose the dream, now at last so nearly realized, of the world set free.

FINIS

Milton Keynes UK
Ingram Content Group UK Ltd.
UKHW011142220424
441551UK00007B/760